PETER GEOGHEGAN is an Irish writer, journalist and broadcaster based in Glasgow. His work has appeared in *The Guardian, The Independent, The London Review of Books, The Times Literary Supplement, The Christian Science Monitor, The Irish Times, Foreign Policy* and numerous other publications. He has reported for Al Jazeera, made documentaries on Mongolian wrestling for BBC Radio 4, spent time reporting from the Balkans and wrote from Egypt during the Arab Spring. He has never been a member of a political party.

From Glasgow's George Square to High Street Stornoway, Peter Geoghegan is an acute, insightful and empathic observer of the referendum campaign and the characters who shaped it. Always questioning, but refreshingly uncynical, his travels through Catalonia, Bosnia and Northern Ireland have given him a unique and challenging perspective on the year that changed Scotland.
LIBBY BROOKS, The Guardian

This book offers a uniquely discursive take on Scotland's referendum experience. While most journalists were tapping official sources, Peter was taking the pulse of ordinary – and not so ordinary – Scots as 18 September approached. The result is a generous, original and distinctive take on Scottish national life.
JAMIE MAXWELL, journalist and commentator

Peter Geoghegan has succinctly and astutely identified the heart of the matter and raised the fundamental question of this campaign, all but missed by the old media: whether or not the momentum in participative democracy will continue after 19 September.
WILL STORRAR, organiser, Bus Party 2013

The
People's Referendum

Why Scotland Will Never Be the Same Again

PETER GEOGHEGAN

Luath Press Limited
EDINBURGH
www.luath.co.uk

For Ealasaid

First published 2015

ISBN: 978-1-910021-52-1

The writer acknowledges the support of

ALBA | CHRUTHACHAIL

towards the writing of this volume.

The paper used in this book is recyclable. It is made from
low chlorine pulps produced in a low energy, low emissions manner
from renewable forests.

Printed and bound by
Bell & Bain Ltd., Glasgow

Typeset in 11.5 point Sabon

Contents

Acknowledgements

This book could not have happened without the help of countless people, many of them complete strangers that I met in villages, towns and cities across Scotland during and after the independence referendum campaign. Some voted Yes, others No, a few were undecided, but they all gave their time freely and generously. They asked for nothing in return, save a fair hearing. I sincerely hope that I have given them that.

I am also indebted to numerous friends and colleagues who offered advice and guidance throughout the writing of this book. I would like in no particular order to record my thanks to Nick Holdstock, Fraser MacDonald, Andrew Tickell, Johnny Rodger, Mitch Miller, David Torrance, Daniel Gray, Dave Scott, Harry Pearson, Aidan Kerr, Evan Beswick, Libby Brooks, Brendan Barrington, Dominic Hinde, Mark Hennessy, Gerry Braiden, David Leask, Feargal Dalton, Jamie Maxwell, Peter Mackay, Liz Castro, William Storrar, Eamonn O'Neill, Iain Macwhirter, Ian Wilson, Ian S. Wood, Iain Pope, Dina Vosanovic, Mary Melvin Geoghegan, Fionnula Mulcahy and Andrew McFadyen. The errors, solecisms and misjudgements within these pages are my entirely my own. Thanks also to Gavin MacDougall and everyone at Luath Press, and to Creative Scotland, who supported this project. Sections of this book are based on writings that previously appeared in *The London Review of Books, The Drouth* and *The Dublin Review*.

A special word of thanks to my family in Ireland, and to Ealasaid, without whose love, support and peerless proofreading skills this book would have remained just another idea in my cluttered filing cabinet.

Finally a note on direct speech quoted in the book. Many of my interviewees spoke in distinctive variations of Scots but due to my own linguistic failings I had to reproduce their words in standard English. My apologies.

Scotland on The Edge

THERE WAS A carnival atmosphere in Glasgow's George Square on Wednesday 17 September 2014. Thousands of Scottish independence supporters filled the square, effectively reclaiming the normally staid collection of worthy statues and grey asphalt as a genuine public space.

A crowd across from the City Chambers chanted 'Scotland' to an off-key tune of 'Hey Jude'. A middle-aged woman meandered slowly through the bodies waving a sign that said 'Scotland don't be scared'. Hipsters with ripped jeans and tattoos walked across the square with Yes stickers in their beards. The unseasonably warm evening leant the whole scene a Mediterranean air. In the gloaming the public address system stopped broadcasting political speeches and began blaring out rave music.

This was Scotland as I had never seen it before. The boisterous rally, organised largely on social media, reminded me of places I had reported from – Cairo's Tahrir Square, Occupy London, restive nights in the Balkans – not the country I had lived in for the best part of a decade. Like the 'occupied' public squares across Europe, the atmosphere was febrile, driven by smart phones and nervous energy. There were similar anxieties, too, about what the following day might bring. Across Scotland, less than 12 hours later, polls would open in the most heavily trailed vote in Scottish history. 'Should Scotland Be An Independent Country?' A Manichean choice. Yes or No.

This book is about how the independence referendum changed not just Scottish politics but the nation's people, its sense of itself and its future. This is the story of the campaign and its aftermath, not as recorded by pollsters and politicians or by the official Yes and No campaigns, Yes Scotland and Better Together, but as it was experienced by some of the five million ordinary – and extraordinary – people involved on both sides of the debate. Their stories also speak to what comes next for Scotland.

Scots said No to independence but a return to the status quo hardly seems possible. Immediately after the referendum, more than 70,000 people joined pro-independence political parties. At the time of writing, in late 2014, the Scottish National Party are riding high in opinion polls both for Holyrood and Westminster. Labour, meanwhile, is trying to re-engage with its core voters, many of whom ignored the party line and said Yes to independence. Among the politicians, the battle for more powers for the devolved parliament at Holyrood was being fought with pens and paper at the cross-party Smith Commission. Most No voters are tired of the constitutional tumult, but for many Yes activists, innervated by the referendum campaign, only full independence will suffice. The future, for Scotland and the UK, has seldom looked more uncertain.

Many commentators outside Scotland struggled to understand why there was a referendum on independence in the first place. Certainly leaving the UK was hardly a burning issue of public concern. Poll after poll put Scottish support for separation at around a third. But, on 5 May 2011, this cosy consensus was broken when the Scottish National Party achieved the seemingly impossible: a majority of seats in the devolved parliament in Edinburgh. A plebiscite on independence was a longstanding manifesto pledge (and for many supporters the party's *raison d'être*). In Westminster, Conservative Prime Minister David Cameron acquiesced to Holyrood's demands. The so-called Edinburgh Agreement was signed the following October. Scotland would have a chance to vote on ending the 1707 Union with England. The eventual result – 55.3 per cent for No; 44.7 for Yes – reaffirmed that Scots favoured the United Kingdom over the establishment of a new state of their own.

But that narrative is too simplistic. The referendum was as much a product of the 2008 financial crash, MPs' expenses, falling real wages and deindustrialisation as it was about commitments laid out in the White Paper, the SNP's prospectus for independence. The gradual erosion of faith in the idea of Great Britain, and Scotland's place in it, began after the Second World War and accelerated in the lugubrious half-light of the 1970s. By the start of the second decade of the new millennium once seemingly immutable Scottish institutions were in chaos, too: the Royal Bank of Scotland, the Catholic Church, Rangers Football Club. The flag waving masses in George Square were a symptom of a wider (partly globalised) malaise, not its root cause. But they were a raucous, often angry indicator all the same. The Glasgow 'occupiers' wanted change – and they saw independence as the best way of getting it.

In George Square on 17 September, as I stood scribbling on the edge of the crowd, a middle-aged woman sidled up to me and asked: 'Are you a journalist?' I nodded, slightly sheepishly. She smiled. 'I just want to talk'. And talk we did. She told me how 'absolutely disgusted' she was by the British political system.

'Not by the UK, not by England, I'm disgusted by Westminster.' She clutched a Saltire by her side. She talked, too, about her brother, who had been killed by an Irish Republican Army sniper in South Armagh during the Troubles.

'He fought and died to protect his people, the people of the UK, a UK he thought was an equal, just country. I don't see how anyone can look at the UK now and say it's any of those things.'

She looked as if she was about to break down in tears. When she had finished she rested an arm on my shoulder, thanked me and, raising her Saltire, disappeared back into crowd from which she had emerged.

Such interactions were largely typical of a referendum debate that was, in the main, remarkably civil. Voices were raised but seldom fists. Quiescence, however, belied the depth of disagreement on both sides about fundamental questions. Among much of the pro-independence Left, the idea that Britain was 'broken' was an article of faith, but for many Scots this was a risible suggestion. Some Scots thought that a new independent state would bring with it a once in a lifetime opportunity to create a fairer country. There were others that worried leaving the UK would see Scotland poorer, more isolated and ruled by a cadre of inferior politicians drawn from a cloistered Central Belt elite. There were a minority who hated the

English, and another rump who saw the Union as a bulwark against Papists and communists. There were some, many even, who did not know what to think and spent two years ingesting information about the pros and cons of leaving the Union before reaching a decision. There were others who made a snap judgment as they stood holding the thin slip of white paper in the voting booth on 18 September. For some the whole gallimaufry was a complete waste of time and money; for others it was a glorious, never-before-glimpsed moment of democratic participation.

The referendum was not just a Scottish affair. The vote begged questions of the rest of the UK too: what would the United Kingdom without Scotland be called? Would it survive as a tripartite union? Who would get the prized family heirlooms, North Sea oil and gas? There could be aftershocks further afield as well. Similar dynamics to those that brought Scotland to a vote on independence are at play in states across Europe, and the world. From Montreal to Antwerp, Venice to Banja Luka, would-be secessionists were watching on with more than dispassionate interest.

In George Square the night before polls opened, four Catalan firefighters encircled an old Seat 600 on the asphalt beside the Cenotaph war memorial. The Seat 600 was the car that had kick-started 'the Spanish miracle', the slow recovery from the vicious civil war years, but these Catalans had come to bury Spain, not praise it.

'We want to give our support to Scotland's referendum and we want the same referendum in Catalonia,' said one of the firefighters as he posed for photographs. He and his friends had driven 1,500 miles from the Catalan city of Girona.

'Maybe it will be easier for us if it is a Yes in Scotland'.

Painted on the bonnet in red and yellow was the *Esteldada*, the starry flag of Catalan *independentistas*. Two months later, I stood in an ad hoc polling station in the Raval neighbourhood of Barcelona as Catalan nationalists held an illegal 'consultation' on independence. People chatted excitedly and took photographs of each other as they cast symbolic ballots. The mood – expectant yet anxious – was not all that different from Glasgow on referendum eve.

Beneath a George Square plinth, as the evening began to draw to a close at around 10.00pm, I ran into a friend, my local SNP councillor Feargal Dalton. Feargal looked exhausted. He had been campaigning hard for months. I knew because I had spent many evenings following him and his gaggle of activists through the cul-de-sacs and closes of Glasgow. Like me, Feargal was born and raised in Ireland before coming to Scotland as an adult. We had last met in an Irish old timers' bar in Partick a few weeks earlier. Feargal had been optimistic that night, but now he was 'nervous', wary of being carried away, of mistaking the rambunctious flag-waving throng for a voting majority. He was right to be circumspect. That the George Square party was more wake than celebration would become clear in the small hours of Friday morning, 19 September, as results began to trickle in from across Scotland. Clackmannanshire, the first count to declare, was a solid no. As was the next, and the next, and the next. There were bright spots for independence supporters (Glasgow and Dundee both voted Yes), but overall Scots elected to stay in the Union by a comfortable margin on a record high turnout. Just shy of 85 per cent of the electorate cast a vote.

Accepting defeat in the early hours of Friday morning, Alex Salmond, SNP leader, Scotland's First Minister and undisputed architect of the referendum, said that the vote had been 'a triumph for the democratic process'. A few hours later, Salmond would announce his intention to step down from the party leadership and the premiership.

David Cameron was 'delighted with the result'. 'There can be no disputes, no re-runs; we have heard the will of the Scottish people,' the British Prime Minister said. A week later, Cameron would be overheard telling former New York Mayor Michael Bloomberg that the Queen had 'purred down the line' when he told her the result.

Independence supporters had declared that there would be a reprise of the party in George Square on Friday morning, to celebrate victory. But at 8.00am there were just a dozen or so young men wrapped in Saltires and strumming guitars underneath the

Scott Monument. Their entire number fitted across a pair of wooden benches. They looked like they had been up all night. A couple supped from cans of beer as the street cleaners hosed down the square around them.

'I'm disappointed. I thought more of Scotland would have said Yes. I'm really upset but what can I do,' said a young man named Martin.

He kept waving his Saltire as he spoke. In the background, international news teams recorded pieces to camera. Later that evening, the square was occupied once again, but this time by hundreds of loyalists. Women in red, white and blue wraparound skirts sang 'you can stuff your independence up your arse'. Sections of the crowd chanted 'Rule Britannia' and 'No Surrender' waving Union flags. A number of independence supporters and non-aligned passers-by were attacked. The referendum was over, but its impact was still being felt.

This is a book about journeys: Scotland's road to referendum day and beyond; the myriad personal and collective excursions taken by people across Scotland during the campaign; and my own personal journey both as a journalist and an emigrant living in Scotland at a momentous moment in the nation's history. 'The referendum is boring' was probably an inevitable cliché in a two-year long campaign but that was seldom my experience. I learned a lot about the arguments for the Union and for independence but I discovered a lot more, too, about the multifarious, often marginalised histories, people and places of what Hugh MacDiarmid (who returns later in this book) recognised as 'our multiform, our infinite Scotland'.

This is not an exhaustive account of what happened in Scotland on 18 September 2014. Instead the book is arranged as a series of essays featuring people, places and issues that animated my own referendum journey – and Scotland's. The chapters that follow explore different themes that played a role in the campaign, from ethnicity and identity to economics and politics. The stories are arranged in loose geographical and chronological order, with each chapter ending with a brief synopsis of the local aftermath of the referendum result. There are frequent diversions into the histories of the places and the people I met, some of which directly relate to the independence debate, some of which form part of the much wider story of what Scotland is now and what it might become.

The book opens in the North Lanarkshire town of Coatbridge, also known as 'Little Ireland'. After spending time with different sides in the splintered debate among the Coatbridge Irish, I move on to a series of journeys to West Fife, to meet ageing communists campaigning for a Yes vote. In 'the Debatable Lands' of the Scottish Borders I found little appetite for independence but discovered revealing cross-border histories. On Lewis, I retraced part of the journey made by another Irishman, Louis MacNeice, on the eve of the Second World War. There are international departures too, to Catalonia and the less familiar Bosnian Serb Republic. Scotland's decision continues to reverberate far beyond the banks of the River Tweed or the choppy waters of the Sea of Moyle. The book ends with a series of accounts from the fevered last month of the campaign, including the contentious subject of the role of the media in the referendum, before closing with a brief summary of the uncertain landscape of Scotland after 18 September 2014.

Any account of such a seismic political and cultural event as Scotland's independence referendum will be partial, only a snapshot of a constantly evolving story. In the immediate post-referendum maelstrom, appearances can be both fleeting and deceiving. The Scottish Labour Party proclaimed 'victory' in the referendum but has since defenestrated its leader and is lagging behind in opinion polls at Westminster and Holyrood. Another name to add to the list of venerable Scottish institutions in turmoil? Perhaps. Both the SNP and the Scottish Greens have more than tripled in size since the vote, adding yet another new dynamic to the political tumult. Among a small section of independence supporters the anger – and the grief – has yet to dissipate. 'The 45', disgruntled *soi-disant* guardians of the Yes flame, are still fighting on, as they see it, against the nefarious

British political class, a biased media, and their timorous compatriots. When, and if, these 21st century Jacobites will lay down their arms is uncertain. Few would bet against another referendum on independence some time in the future. One thing seems assured: the referendum on 18 September 2014 changed Scotland, perhaps forever.

Peter Geoghegan
Glasgow
October 2014

www.petergeoghegan.com
@peterkgeoghegan

CHAPTER ONE

Big Debate in Little Ireland

The Scotch and Irish friendly are
Their wishes are the same,
The English nation envy us,
And over us would reign.
Our historians and our poets
They always did maintain,
That the origins of Scottish men and Irish were the same.

HENRY JOY MCCRACKEN, 18th-century Belfast revolutionary

COATBRIDGE LOOKS like just about any other post-industrial town in Scotland's Central Belt. A flat, manmade horizon punctured by vertiginous multi-storey council flats. Row upon row of post-war terraced houses studded with pebbledash. An unremarkable main street lined with chain stores and charity shops. But Coatbridge has a distinctive place in Scottish life, and especially in the lives of the hundreds of thousands of Scots whose Irish heritage is a formative part of how they view themselves.

Coatbridge is often called 'Little Ireland'. In the middle of the 19th century, thousands of Irish emigrants arrived in Glasgow, their search for work often ending in North Lanarkshire where many Irish men and women found employment in the hulking blast furnaces of 'the Iron Burgh'. These workers lived and died in dilapidated hovels in wards with names like 'Paddy's Land' and 'Irish Land'. At the time, the *Glasgow Free Press* called Coatbridge and Airdrie 'the nearest thing possible to two Irish colonies'. The steelworks are gone, but today some 70 per cent of residents can trace their ancestry back to Ireland. Almost every Coatbridge surname arrives flecked with the swash of the Irish Sea. Locals speak of Donegal and Derry, Mayo and Monaghan, with an affection and intimacy that belies their geographical remove. This town of around

40,000, ten miles east of Glasgow, boasts a Gaelic football team, Irish dancing schools, ten Catholic churches and Irish republican flute bands that march every summer in Belfast. As in the North of Ireland, there are even splinter bands opposed to the peace process.

Such enthusiastic expressions of Irishness never appealed to me much. In almost a decade living in Scotland, I tended to avoid Celtic matches and Irish pubs. I preferred the story I told myself about my own identity: I had come to Scotland of my own volition, not to work all day in soot and smoke but on a university scholarship. Ireland was an hour and a budget flight away, not an active part of my life in Scotland. But over time these purely personal narratives became harder to sustain. When I moved to Glasgow a couple of years ago the 'where are you from?' questions became more frequent, more inflected. Some wanted to claim my Irishness, others to traduce it. As Marx succinctly put it, we make our own histories in circumstances 'given and transmitted from the past'. The history of the Irish in Scotland shades my own experiences. Which, perhaps, partly explains why stepping off the train at Coatbridge's incongruously named Sunnyside station for the first time felt like being transported back home. It was a dreich Sunday evening in early March. Shards of rain pierced a dark sky. Overhead sodium streetlights emitted a rheumy yellow glare. Ahead of me, a man in his early 20s in tracksuit bottoms and a hooded top ducked into a grey, breezeblock building. Above the doorway a Union Flag fluttered in the breeze. The remains of red, white and blue bunting clung to a drainpipe. Below a pair of middle-aged men and a slightly older women stood and smoked. This, as I was later to learn, was the local Orange Hall.

I had come to Coatbridge for a debate about the Irish in Scotland and the independence referendum as part of the 12th annual St Patrick's Day Festival (which, despite the name, lasted for two weeks). The discussion was being held in a community centre in the shadow of St Patrick's Catholic Church. Across the road, cardboard cut-out shamrocks were stuck to the inside windows of a busy bar. The community centre was warm and clammy inside. On the walls hung prints of a beatific St Patrick and a hirsute Jesus Christ. The latter had the same penetrating stare as the devotional painting that used to sit above the spare bed in my grandfather's house in Dublin. On the stage, empty plastic chairs were lined up in front of two long tables, ready for the speakers. Behind the platform was a banner with an Irish Tricolour: 'Céad míle fáilte'. Half a dozen members of the Coatbridge St Patrick's Day committee milled around.

'There was a sense before in which you kept your Irishness under your hat,' Tom Nolan, the festival chair told me over a ham sandwich and a cup of milky tea. 'Is it not about time we could celebrate our culture?' Nolan had a soft, friendly face and wore a green Gaelic football jersey with a Celtic cross on the crest.

As we spoke a heavyset man arrived, slightly out of breath. He was just back from watching local side Albion Rovers taking on the once mighty Rangers in the Scottish Cup at Ibrox. The Coatbridge outfit are amongst the least successful senior sides in Scotland. (The Cliftonhill side last played in the top flight in 1948–49. They picked up the princely total of eight points.) At Ibrox, they had come within 12 minutes of a famous victory before conceding a late penalty: 'It was never a penalty kick. If they weren't Rangers they never would have got it.' The match finished one-all. For many Irish Catholics in Scotland, Rangers is the embodiment of a nefarious, omnipotent Protestant establishment that permeates Scottish society. While some took Rangers' inglorious bankruptcy in 2012 as evidence that sectarianism was fading away, others still see anti-Catholic bigotry at almost every turn. The following night a prominent anti-Rangers blogger was to appear as part of the St Patrick's Festival. His talk was already sold out.

The independence referendum debate was popular, too. At least 100 people were crowded into the low-ceilinged function room. Before the discussion started Tom Nolan sat on the stage drawing salmon pink and white raffle tickets from a plastic bag. Winners were called out on a crackly microphone. Father Sweeney, the white-haired local parish priest, stood at the back of the hall, surveying the scene from over his glasses. It felt like a hazy memory from the Ireland of my youth. Middle-aged men drank pints of Guinness and talked loudly about football and politics. All that was missing was red lemonade and Tayto crisps. The compere introduced each of the eight speakers by their ancestral homeplaces. I imagined some putative descendent of mine being described as 'his family on his father's side hailed from County Longford'. The thought did not fill me with cheer. The final announcement, that the bar would be closed throughout the discussion, brought the biggest response of the evening, a knowingly loud collective groan.

Earlier, Tom Nolan had told me that the prospect of Scottish independence 'divided' Irish Catholics in Coatbridge.

'There is a school of thought that says you should definitely vote No because there is an underlying anti-Irish racism,' he said in a slow, considered voice. 'There is a republican element that thinks independence is absolutely right and there is an element that is a bit confused about what would happen with independence.'

The debate would turn into a clash between all three positions. Professor Tom Devine – who would declare his own support for independence later in the year – said that Catholics were more likely to vote Yes than any other group in Scottish society.

'A mere 16 per cent were very concerned about the possibility of an independent Scotland,' said Devine, quoting recent surveys of social attitudes. A Labour member of the Scottish Parliament (MSP) seated nearby shook his head vigorously: 'no, no, that's not true'. Another Labour MSP cited polling that suggested Scottish National Party supporters wanted to close Catholic schools – a shibboleth in places like Coatbridge. The discussion spiralled off in discordant directions: the controversial 2012 Offensive Behaviour Football Bill that had led to the arrest of Celtic fans for the most minor of infringements; whether Scottish independence might lead to a united Ireland; how best to protect Catholic education. One speaker, a retired academic, complained about 'gay rights propaganda' in schools.

From the floor, Tom Clarke, Labour MP for Coatbridge since 1982, said independence would leave Scotland – and the Irish community – poorer and more vulnerable. His voice was loud and confident. Nearby a red-faced man started shouting about Tony Blair and Labour's role in the 2003 invasion of Iraq. As the evening wore on, Devine looked increasingly weary. The brow above his dark sunglasses furrowed ever deeper and I thought I could hear his sighs from my seat near the stage. I sympathised. It seemed as if most of the audience – and some of the speakers – saw themselves as members of an embattled tribe, assailed on all sides by hostile forces. Unguarded, the Irish Catholic way of life in Scotland would be trampled on and eradicated. I did not share their fears but I could understand them. When the place you live in is dubbed 'the least Scottish town in Scotland' – as Coatbridge was by the Times in 2006 – it is hard not to feel like outsiders, even if your antecedents had lived for generations among the one-time mining towns and steel mills of North Lanarkshire. Scotland has not always been good to 'Little Ireland'.

It was still raining when I arrived back at Sunnyside train station. One of the speakers from the debate, the youngest on the panel, was sitting on a bench, sheltering as best he could from the elements.

'That was a waste of time,' he said and looked fed up. With six months to go to the referendum he had wanted to talk about independence, not Catholic schools. 'But they're hypersensitive in Coatbridge.' We sat together on the train to Glasgow. A little further down the carriage, a man of around 30 was talking loudly into a mobile phone. He had a broad Dublin accent. On the lapel of his bomber jacket was an Easter lily pin, an Irish republican symbol of remembrance for those killed on 'active service'.

* * *

Just 12 miles separate Scotland and Ireland at the narrowest point. Some days during the independence referendum, the distance between the Mull of Kintyre and Fair Head felt like a mere hop, but on most, the two lands seemed worlds apart.

Throughout the campaign Scottish nationalists frequently cited Ireland as a model of how to sever the British Union, but rarely thought through the lessons on everything from sovereignty and citizenship to currency and border controls to be learned from post-1922 Dublin. On the other side of the constitutional divide, over 10,000 Orangemen marched through Edinburgh just five days before the referendum. It was the largest Orange parade in Scotland in living memory, reported on the top of that evening's BBC network news as a huge 'pro-Union rally'.

Across the Straits of Moyle, the attitude was similarly ambivalent. In Northern Ireland, nationalists – wary of adding a religious element to avowedly secular Scottish nationalism – were muted about the possibility of the break-up of Britain. Some excitable unionists warned that a Yes vote in Scotland could spark a return to violence on the streets of Belfast. In Dublin, government ministers were told to remain studiously neutral on 'the Scottish Question'.

Scotland and Ireland were not always this removed from each other's affairs. Back in the 6th century, parts of both were encompassed within the Dalriadic kingdom. Dalriada, which stretched from Argyll to Antrim, was, in the words of Neal Ascherson, 'A Gaelic-speaking Atlantic world connected rather than divided by the sea.' Among those who lived in Dalriada was possibly the most famous of all Irish migrants to Scotland: St Columba. As a tempestuous young monk, Columba became embroiled in an increasingly violent quarrel over the copying of a manuscript. The squabble, cited by some as the world's first copyright dispute, led eventually to Columba's exile. He was ordered to atone for his sins by becoming a missionary beyond the sea. He was to go north until he could no longer see Ireland. Legend has it that he travelled in a wicker coracle covered with leather, stopping first at the tip of the Mull of Kintyre. But he could see the cliffs of Antrim, so he set off again. Next he landed on the Sound of Jura. But even there he could glimpse his homeland in the distance. Columba and his companions eventually settled on Iona. They climbed Dun I, the island's little hill, and made a cairn of stones. They named it *Carn cul ri Erin* ('The Cairn of the Back Turned to Ireland').

Columba and Iona remain pivotal episodes in the story of Christianity in Scotland. In 1938, a Church of Scotland minister in Govan named George MacLeod established the Iona Community, initially to rebuild the ruined medieval abbey. The Iona Community is now an ecumenical centre, attracting pilgrims from around the world. But the story of Dalriada has largely been forgotten. This neglect began after the Reformation, when anything redolent of Ireland gave off the unseemly whiff of Catholicism. There was little appetite for talk of an overland Gaelic kingdom joining Ireland and Scotland.

Indeed, the broader story of Scotland and Ireland has often been reduced to religion. The reason for this largely lies in a series of political events that cut to the quick of relations between Scotland, Ireland and Ulster – the Acts of Union.

Ostensibly the 1707 and 1801 Acts of Union were broadly similar. Both bound smaller polities into an alliance with a larger, more powerful and richer neighbour. They were not the product of popular consultation or democratic will; neither were they opposed by significant violence at the time of their passage. But the two unions were – and are – very different. The 1707 union was a compromise. Scotland retained its own systems of law and local government, its own parish schools and universities, its own forms of church government. Scotland, in sum, held on to a sense of itself as a separate nation within a union that it had willingly joined and which it measured the success of, almost singularly, in material gain. The situation in Ireland was very different. Ireland was in many important respects a British colony. Many Catholics felt minimal attachment to the British state and, as the famine attested, the British state felt minimal attachment to them. This religious distinction was hardly accidental. The United Kingdom was created as a counterpoint to largely Catholic continental Europe. In Protestant Britain, papists represented the dangerous 'Other': lazy, feckless, a fifth column in waiting. Such 'assertions of blessed Protestant insularity', wrote Linda Colley, 'remained widespread far into the 20th century'.

Protestantism underpinned one of the largest movements of people between Scotland and Ireland: the Ulster Plantations. Between 1650 and 1700, anywhere between 60,000 and 100,000 Scots (many of them Presbyterians) travelled across the narrow stretch of clear blue water to start a new life in the glens of Ulster. This migration was not all one-way. In 1841, the Irish-born population of Scotland stood at 126,321, or 4.8 per cent of the population. Ten years later it was 207,367. Most of these new migrants were Catholic. Many climbed off over-crowded ships at the Brommielaw in Glasgow, before travelling on to the towns of industrial Scotland, such as Coatbridge, where there were opportunities in the factories powering the empire. Discrimination was rife. In 1923, the Presbytery of Glasgow & The Synod of Glasgow and Ayr presented a report to the General Assembly of the Kirk on the *Menace of the Irish Race to our Scottish Nationality*.

There was another aspect of Irish emigration to Scotland in the 18th and 19th centuries – Irish Protestants. During the Napoleonic Wars many Ulster Protestants left for Scotland, where economic opportunities and wages were increasing much faster. Protestants accounted for somewhere between a quarter and a fifth of emigrants from Ireland to Scotland, a trend that only declined in the late 19th and early 20th centuries. Some brought with them the nascent creed of Orangeism. The Orange Order in Scotland still draws a substantial amount of its support from descendants of these Ulster emigrants. As historian Graham Walker wrote:

> Orange songs and banners and slogans spell out the claim to an indivisible bond between Scotland and Ulster for those who desire, or think it important, to hear it.

Most Irish Protestants eventually assimilated into mainstream Scottish society. The experience of Irish Catholics was rather different. While the sun eventually set on the British Empire, Scotland's Irish

Catholic community remained as a colonial vestige, dwelling not in the far-flung periphery but in the metropolitan heartland. The on-going conflict in Northern Ireland put further strains on the relationship with the 'indigenous' community, particularly in part of the West of Scotland that had also experienced significant historic Protestant migration from Ulster.

Sectarianism was long a feature of everyday Scottish life. Catholic Scots only achieved occupational parity in the 1990s. While overt discrimination has been on the wane, there has been a marked increase in interest in sectarianism in Scotland. Recent years has brought controversial anti-sectarian legislation and endless column inches dedicated to 'Scotland's shame'. But whether sectarianism is a still significant part of the Irish Catholic experience, or, as empirical evidence would seem to suggest, fast diminishing, the very fact that Scotland is still so preoccupied with issues of religious difference attests to a sense of separateness that many Irish Catholics in Scotland still feel.

Scotland and Ireland were pushed further apart amid the political and economic tumult of the industrial revolution. Campaigns first for Catholic Emancipation and later Irish Home Rule existed largely in isolation from political reform initiatives in Scotland. But there were radical, even revolutionary, connections between the two nations, too. Henry Joy McCracken and the United Irishmen led the 1798 rebellion in Ireland on a platform of uniting 'Protestant, Catholic and Dissenter'. The Irishmen failed but they did provide the inspiration – and the constitution – for the United Scotsmen, a republican secret society whose members included weavers, pedlars and seasonal harvesters that left Ulster for Scotland. In the late 19th century, John Ferguson, a Protestant Ulsterman, was a moving spirit in the Irish National Land League in Glasgow. In January 1913, a Scottish Presbyterian named Douglas Hogg stood in a by-election in Derry City on a Home Rule platform. *The Belfast Weekly* pilloried him as 'the Scottish Lundy'. There are few graver calumnies in Protestant Ulster. Every year, the Apprentice Boys of Derry burn an effigy of Robert Lundy, the Protestant leader accused of betraying the city during 1688 Siege of Derry. Hogg held on to win the seat, with a majority of 57.

Such connections between Scotland, Ireland and Ulster extended beyond the urban milieu. Raasay-born poet Sorley MacLean envisaged Gaelic Scotland and Ireland as part of a single cultural continuity. Like Scotland and Ireland more generally, Gaelic literature was once closely connected, but was subsequently, as contemporary Scottish Gaelic poet Peter Mackay noted, 'divided by differences in language, historical context and political status'. Educational and cultural support has saved Scottish Gaelic from what Norman Davies called 'its second death'. Links with the Irish language are now arguably closer than at anytime since the 1940s. At the same time, Scots speakers have often been involved in the Ulster Scots movement in the North of Ireland.

Political relations between Scotland and Ireland have changed, too. The restive North is not the thorn in the Celtic side it once was. While Arthur Aughey may be right to say that Scots keep Northern Ireland 'at a safe distance', journalist David Torrance quotes an unnamed SNP source as saying that the Good Friday Agreement was 'hugely influential' to Scottish nationalist thinking, showing what could be achieved by moderation and pragmatism.

The success of the SNP also reflects the decline of once powerful unifying narratives of British identity. Scotland and Ireland have differing relationships with the very idea of Britain. Catholics in Ireland tend to view Britishness as something foreign, to be disavowed; for Northern Irish Protestants it is existential and constitutive. For most Scots, however, the relationship has long been far more utilitarian and transactional. 'What does the Union do for me?' 'Am I better off within or without?' That was the ground upon which the independence referendum was fought – and eventually won – but this narrow vista largely ignored a once voluble section of Scottish society: those for whom Protestant Britishness remains an integral part of their sense of identity.

* * *

There was serious rioting in the town of Coatbridge, Lanark County, Scotland, Saturday, between parties of Orangemen and Catholics, when 26 of the participants in the disturbance were arrested. Two police officers were dangerously wounded in quelling the disorder. The rioting was resumed this morning, when a number of Catholics, armed with picks and hammers, paraded the main street of the town in search of their religious antagonists, and resisted the efforts of a force of police sent to disperse them... The town is in great excitement as fresh trouble is expected.

The New York Times, 21 August 1883

Coatbridge Orange Hall looked as austere on a Monday afternoon ten days before the referendum as it had when I first passed it on my way to the St Patrick's debate six months earlier. The squat, two-storey building had the neat pyramidal form of a small church, but was unflatteringly finished in breezeblock concrete. The featureless grey façade mirrored the overcast sky. There was a streaky mark on the only window that looked on to the street.

'That's just an egg,' said Jim McDonald, local Orangeman and my guide for the day as he opened the heavy wooden front door and led me into the reception. A homemade poster beside the fruit machine advertised the following week's 'Red, White and Blue Sash Bash'. On the opposite wall, a banner declared that 'Scotland Says No to Separatism'. Its visual language was confusing. Scotland was represented as a Saltire jigsaw piece that had already come loose from a quartet of tiles, each bearing one of the flags of the three other home nations and the Union itself. The graphic seemed to imply that Scotland had already broken away from the rest of the UK.

The Orange Hall was busy. In the large function hall a dozen or so elderly women sat eating sandwiches and drinking tea from glass cups. Their weekly bingo session was due to start shortly. I gave a loud, smiling 'Hello'. Almost everyone waved back.

'A lot of people think it's just the big drum and the Twelfth of July but I could be in this hall three or four times a week for different activities,' said McDonald. A small man in his late-60s, he wore a Rangers pin and a badge for Better Together, the No campaign, on his jacket. He was retired but had worked as an engineer in a local steelworks. When that closed in 1990 he became a postal worker. The following month he would celebrate half a century in the Coatbridge Orange Order ('I'll be getting my medal').

Unbidden, McDonald gave me a tour of the walls of the hall. There were prints of William of Orange – 'King Billy' – on his steed and faded framed photographs of the Queen flanked by the Duke of Edinburgh and a yellowish Queen Mother. There were pictures, too, of lines of Orangemen in black suits and white gloves standing to attention.

'That's the Loyal Sons of Ulster,' McDonald pointed up at a semi-circle of broad-shouldered, middle-aged men. They looked mostly plump and contented. Established in 1906, the Loyal Sons are one of more than ten lodges affiliated to Coatbridge Orange Hall. All the founder members were Ulsterman.

McDonald led me on to a plague framed in gold that recorded past district masters dating back to 1865.

'He was an Ulsterman,' McDonald jabbed a finger at one of the first names on the dark wood board. 'He was an Ulsterman.' He pointed, too quickly, at another. 'He was an Ulsterman'. I only caught one name. William Whitelaw. He was an ancestor of Willie Whitelaw who, amongst other things, was Secretary of State for Northern Ireland in the early 1970s, during some of the worst violence of the Troubles. Margaret Thatcher would later tell MPs, 'every prime minister needs a Willie'.

McDonald was descended from Irish stock, too. The absence of Protestants from the local green-tinged festivities was a source of grievance.

'If you mention Coatbridge to anyone they just think Roman Catholic. They had a St Patrick's Day festival for a week but it's all Roman Catholic,' he said. 'There was nothing from the unionist side, just Celtic and Tricolours'.

Earlier, as we walked up from the train station past rows of council flats, he had complained that Catholics received preferential access to housing. Religion has often been said to play a significant role in the politics of Coatbridge and the surrounding areas; the SNP were accused of playing the sectarian card during the 1994 Monklands by-election when their campaign focused heavily on discrepancies in spending by the local Labour administration that appeared to favour Catholic Coatbridge over its largely Protestant neighbour Airdrie.

Jim McDonald led me to a small meeting room on the second floor of the Orange Hall. On a table inside was a sheaf of papers, including a photocopy of a clipping from the *Airdrie and Coatbridge Advertiser* dated September 1912. Above a notice about a boy scouts' parade was a slightly larger classified ad. 'Copies of the Solemn League and Covenant can be signed at the Conservative Club on Church Street', it declared in serif font. 'Support Loyal Ulster'. Irish Protestant anti-Home Rulers drew up the 'Ulster Covenant', the name consciously echoing the 17th century Presbyterian Covenant-ers that fermented rebellion across the Lowlands and beyond. On Ulster Day, 28 September 1912, around half a million signed the Covenant. Only those who were natives of Ulster were eligible to put their names to the declaration. Addresses of relatives or friends had to be proffered as proof. In Coatbridge alone, 860 men and 96 women put their names to the Covenant. McDonald's paternal grandfather, a bricklayer called James, gave an address on Sandy Row, a famously loyalist south Belfast neighbourhood, although he had been born and raised in Scotland not Ulster. ('He cheated a bit,' his grandson said.) McDonald followed this grandfather – and later his own father – into the Orange Order.

McDonald had all the virtues of the best kind of amateur historian: methodical, knowledgeable and patient of the uninitiated. After I had finished reading the Covenant, he took a scrap of paper out of his pocket. Written in blue biro in capital letters were the names of all Coatbridge Orangemen who died in the First World War. The screed was covered in ink. Among the names was Thomas Dickson, the son of his paternal great grandfather, also Thomas Dickson, who came from Ballynahinch in County Down to work as a blast furnace filler in William Baird's steel works in Coatbridge. Baird was a canny mogul. As well as supplying the land for the local Catholic Church and its Church of Scotland equivalent, he also provided a plot for the Orange Hall in which we sat. 'He had to look after his workers on both sides,' McDonald smiled.

The Grand Orange Lodge was once a powerful political force in Scotland, particularly in the west coast where the large Irish immigrant community comprised both Irish Protestants and Catholics. In the 1920s, the Order claimed a Scottish membership in the hundreds of thousands, including then Tory Secretary of State for Scotland Sir John Gilmour (who repudiated the 1923 *Menace* report about the Irish in Scotland). The Order's membership has fallen sharply since then but there are still over 180 lodges in the Glasgow area alone. Around 8,000 people attend the annual Orange Walk in the city, held ahead of the Twelfth of July parades in Northern Ireland. The Order was traditionally aligned with the Scottish Conservative and Unionist Party but this dynamic shifted in step with the electoral demise of the Tories in Scotland. Scottish Orangeism today is a largely working-class creed. Many Orangemen vote Labour. But the Union is the cause dearest to the hearts of most members.

The Orange Order was effectively barred from joining Better Together. Instead the Order formed its own pro-Union campaign, British Together, which on occasion attracted a level of support from fringe far-right groups. On social media a thoughtful, prolific Twitter account bearing the almost oxymoronic handle 'Orangemen4Indy' provided an Orange-tinged case for independence, but this lively feed was hardly representative of the bulk of the membership.

'The majority of us are voting No. I don't think anyone would expect the Orange Order to vote any other way because of our allegiance to the Queen,' said Jim McDonald when I asked about the referendum. On a nearby wall, a youthful looking Queen Elizabeth II smiled down. Beside us a blind was drawn across the round window that looked out on the street. The shade was white

Window blind, Coatbridge Orange Hall

with a colourful motif: a crown, an open Bible and King Billy's motto, 'This We Will Maintain'.

I visited Coatbridge Orange Hall a day after an opinion poll in *The Times* had given Yes a two-point lead. Jim McDonald said he was 'a bit worried' about how the referendum was shaping up. We climbed up a short ladder into the hall's dusty, narrow attic to admire the Lodge's flags and standards. There was a bright Orange banner with a figure of King Billy, sword raised, and another with a Bible scene, Christ surrounded by children. A cushioned red box about a foot wide lay on the ground. This would hold the Bible at the front of an Orange procession. It was covered in protective plastic with 'LOL No 8' scribbled in pen across it. A padlock barred the way to a separate, smaller room where the bands' instruments were kept. They would be needed that weekend. Most of the Coatbridge lodges were participating in the massive Edinburgh parade calling for a No vote. Orangemen from across the UK were coming to join. McDonald's friend Dawson Bailie, former Grand Master of the Belfast Lodge, was travelling over.

'If it was a Yes vote what would happen in Northern Ireland? Would Sinn Fein want a vote to separate in Ireland, too?' He sounded genuinely concerned.

After clambering down from the attic, I went back into the main hall to say goodbye to the ladies. Their bingo session over, they sat drinking tea and talking in low voices. Near the door was a framed sign that said all functions must close by 'standing for the rendering of the National Anthem'. Failure to do so would result in suspension 'Sine Die'. Jim McDonald looked deflated when I asked what they would sing if there was a Yes vote.

'If we go independent I don't know what national anthem we'll use.'

About a mile or so from Coatbridge Orange Hall, the green, white and gold of the Irish Tricolour hung above a small storefront. Metal bars ran across the windows. I stood peering in, past adverts for a new book by former IRA gunman-cum-Stormont Minister Gerry Kelly and a sign advertising 'the Hunger Strike Raffle'. Sinn Fein President Gerry Adams smiled down from a large placard that took up almost the entire right-hand window. The name Margaret Skinnider hung above the door.

Margaret Skinnider was born on Main Street, Coatbridge in 1892. Twenty-four years later, she fought in the Easter Rising in Dublin. She survived, the only woman wounded in combat in the failed rebellion that – unwittingly – spawned the war that led to Ireland's independence. Skinnider died in Dublin in 1971. In Coatbridge she gives her name to the headquarters of Cairde na hÉireann, the largest Irish republican organisation in Scotland.

As I stood squinting into the narrow, dark shop front, a tall, broad-shouldered young man with short hair and acne scars arrived to let me in. Inside was like a republican Belfast version of the shortbread and tartan tourist traps on Edinburgh's Royal Mile. James Connolly and Bobby Sands smiled down from t-shirt racks. Provisionals' Gaelic games jerseys, Palestinian flags and copies of the proclamation of Ireland and the Sinn Fein newspaper *An Phoblacht* were all on sale. There were H Blocks pins

Window, Skinnider Centre, Coatbridge

and books about De Valera and Michael Collins in the communal library. Staffed entirely by volunteers, the shop opened Friday through Sunday. A republican flute band is based in the centre but much of the energy now goes into running a food bank.

In 2013, unemployment in North Lanarkshire was 20 per cent above the Scottish average. The young man who slipped a key into the padlocked door ran the food bank. He was serious and diligent and talked about the organisation's 'responsibilities to the community' as he showed me shelves filled with toilet paper and tins of beans. He asked more than once that I did not use his name. He was, he said, worried about being targeted by local loyalists.

Irish republicanism has a long history in Coatbridge. In 1919, as the War of Independence was escalating in Ireland, Sinn Fein had three branches in the town. In the 1950 general election the tiny Irish Anti-Partition League ran a candidate in the town. The violence in Northern Ireland never spilled over into armed sectarian conflict in Scotland, but the Troubles did resonate across the Sea of Moyle. Tensions were not confined to Old Firm clashes. A group called the Young Scottish Loyalists had a paid up membership of 1,500 in 1982. A few years earlier, the first republican band in Coatbridge, the James Connolly Republican Flute Band, was established. Clashes between loyalists and republicans were common in Coatbridge.

Cairde na hÉireann – 'friends of Ireland' – was set up after the Northern Irish peace process, around the turn of the millennium, 'because of the needs for a political organisation given the end of the armed struggled and the need to unite Ireland politically' said Franny McAdam, a 48-year-old Coatbridge taxi driver and Cairde na hÉireann's national organiser. Out of a Scottish membership of 600, some 70 are in Coatbridge. In the back room of the Skinnider Centre, sun-bleached photographs of marchers in Belfast with 1980s haircuts were stuck to the walls. Some were sun bleached. Every year Coatbridge holds the biggest republican march in Scotland.

'Cairde na hÉireann could have hundred and hundreds of members here but we don't allow anyone in who does drugs or engages in anti-social behaviour,' said McAdam. The young man who ran the food bank nodded briskly.

Why, I asked, did so many people in a Scottish town take such a passionate interest in a place that, for some, their grandparents and even great grandparents were born? McAdam looked a bit surprised at the question, but answered nonetheless.

'Scotland never embraced the Irish. It actively stopped the Irish from voting. I know people who dropped the 'O' off their name just to get jobs. If the Scottish had embraced the Irish we would probably feel more Scottish.'

For most of the 20th century, Irish Catholics were generally wary of Scottish nationalism. At the 1974 general election the SNP won 30 per cent, but less than one in ten Catholics voted nationalist. That has changed dramatically. Irish Catholics are no longer the reliable bedrock of the Scottish Labour Party; the 2011 Holyrood elections was the first time more Catholics voted SNP than Labour.

There were no Saltires or Yes stickers in the Skinnider Centre, but there was no doubting where the referendum loyalties lay.

'I believe the Scottish people have the right to self-determination as well as the Irish people,' said McAdam. 'Obviously as republicans we would like to see the break-up of the Union.'

* * *

Around lunchtime on 18 September, I walked for a quarter of an hour from Sunnyside station to one of the main Coatbridge polling stations, housed inside a local sports complex. Along the way, I passed a white van covered in Yes stickers. Nearby an elderly man in a Union Flag t-shirt talked loudly about why 'independence would be a disaster'. On the corner of the main street, in an imperious three-storey red sandstone building with a white turret, was the local branch of Airdrie Savings Bank, the only independent saving bank left in the whole of the UK. The 2008 banking crisis was a direct result of the concentration of financial power into a handful of super-sized institutions. As some leftwing independence campaigners were fond of pointing out, little has changed in the intervening years. The big banks are largely intact and Britain remains worryingly dependent on financial services, overwhelmingly based in London.

Outside the polling station, I met the young man from the Skinnider Centre. He was wearing a Yes badge and handing out literature to the occasional voter that floated past from the nearby pebbledash encrusted council flats.

'I'm feeling confident,' he flashed a youthful smile. 'I think we can do it.'

Inside, in a wood-panelled sports hall, an election official said that turnout was unprecedented. By lunchtime more than a quarter of those on the roll had voted. 'Whatever happens I just hope these people keep voting,' she said.

By the next morning all the results were in. North Lanarkshire was one of just four councils in Scotland that voted Yes. In Zone B, the electoral area encompassing Coatbridge, the result was 30,065 in favour of independence and 26,903 against. A week or so after the referendum, I called Jim McDonald. He was pleased with the outcome.

'I think the parade in Edinburgh swayed the vote. That and Gordon Brown.'

CHAPTER TWO

From Rosyth with Love

ON 23 JANUARY 2014 a by-election was held for the Scottish Parliament seat of Cowdenbeath. At around noon, Alex Rowley, the Labour candidate and firm favourite, sat hunched over a plastic-topped table in the café area of the Benarty Community Centre, on the eastern lip of the Fife constituency. A red rosette was pinned to the lapel of his double-breasted brown car coat.

An eager Scottish media had framed the Cowdenbeath by-election as an early bellwether for September's referendum. A Scottish National Party breakthrough in a safe Labour seat would signal the imminent break-up of Britain; conversely, the logic ran, a convincing win for Rowley would send unionists into the spring with renewed confidence that the independence bid would fail.

In the run-up to the vote, newspapers regularly referred to Cowdenbeath as a 'Labour heartland', a phrase once used to describe most of post-industrial Scotland but that has become increasingly redundant. The Scottish National Party, however, does still struggle to make significant inroads among the pit villages that ribbon through the low hills of West Fife. Labour holds the majority of seats on the local council. Cowdenbeath forms part of former Prime Minister Gordon Brown's Westminster constituency. For decades, the greatest threat to Labour's electoral supremacy here came not from the nationalists, but the communists. The area returned Britain's last Communist MP, Willie Gallacher, between 1935 and 1950. In 1973, the Communist Party of Great Britain won 12 council seats in Lochgelly and Cowdenbeath. Among those elected was Willie Clarke.

More than 40 years later, Willie Clarke is still a local councillor for Ballingry, the small town of post-war suburban pebbledash terraces laid out on the escarpment of Benarty Hill. A broad-shouldered, craggy-faced septuagenarian, Clarke has been called 'the last

Communist councillor in Britain', although technically he has been an independent for most of the last two decades. In Fife's last local elections in 2012, Clarke was returned in The Lochs ward in the first round of voting. There was, as usual, no Communist candidate on the January by-election ballot paper, but Clarke had come to the Benarty Centre that morning to watch proceedings.

'Hello, Comrade,' Alex Rowley lifted his right hand in greeting when their eyes met. Over the previous half hour a steady trickle of people had filed through the centre's automatic glass double doors, past the reception desk and into the main hall that was serving as a polling station for the day.

'Lots of folk out today. You'll do well.' Willie Clarke spoke slowly, in a low voice delivered out of the right hand corner of his month. In late 2011, he lost his left ear to cancer. The operation left him with a pronounced scar and little control over one side of his face.

'Hopefully, hopefully.' Rowley gently shifted his weight from one foot to the other. During Clarke's seven weeks in Edinburgh Western General recuperating from his surgery, he would often wake during the night to find Rowley, then leader of Fife Council, sitting by his bedside.

'You'll be fine. You'll win.' Willie Clarke gave a smile of reassurance and brushed a few long white hairs across his forehead. Thick eyebrows framed his dark green-blue eyes. Rowley rested his hand on Clarke's shoulder for a moment.

'Farewell,' the Labour candidate said before walking out into a bright, but bracing, winter morning. Two middle-aged men with clipboards followed in consort. Across the street, the canary yellow of a pair of SNP canvassers twinkled in the sunlight. In the middle distance, past some houses and a factory, a troop of wind turbines rotated slowly on the hills.

An hour or so later, Clarke pulled up outside a fishing tackle shop in Cowdenbeath. Across the road, a gentle slope led to the train platform. He apologised for not spending the whole day with me,

By-election day, Cowdenbeath

but that afternoon he had to speak at the funeral of an 88-year-old communist in Kirkcaldy. As I put my notebook in my bag, I asked how he would be voting in the referendum. He cleared his throat.

'I hope that Scotland votes for independence because that would be a day I'd cherish for the rest of my life.'

His voice rose, shaking slightly as it did so. Each sentence started slowly, almost gently, but built up into a forceful finale. It sounded like an oration he had delivered before.

'Independence will come, whether it comes the now or in 20 years, it's like the tide you cannot hold it back, it's going to happen. People will have to look at what is going to provide a fairer society, and it's certainly not the capitalist system.'

Over the next eight months, Clarke would become one of the most active independence campaigners in his corner of Fife, facilitating meetings and debates, canvasses and leaflet drops. The Communist Party had disappeared but some of its fabled discipline and organisational nous remained in West Fife.

* * *

At the end of the Second World War, membership of the Communist Party of Great Britain (CPGB) stood at just over 50,000. This was far less than its sister parties in France and Italy, but enough to give it genuine electoral clout. In the 1945 general election, Communists won two seats, with Willie Gallacher successfully holding West Fife against strong Labour opposition. In local elections the following year, the number of Communist councillors increased from 81 to 215. This was to prove a high-water mark for the CPGB. By the time Russian tanks rolled into Budapest in 1956, it had already lost all its representation at Westminster. In the wake of the brutal suppression of the revolution in Hungary – which the party's organ, *The Morning Star*, refused to report on – the party haemorrhaged members. They would never return. Nevertheless, the Communists remained a presence in outposts of industrial Britain, in South Wales, East London, and in the coalfields of Fife and Ayrshire. Communists were prominent in Scottish trades councils, too, particularly in the National Union of Mineworkers. The communist influence within the Scottish Trades Union Congress (STUC) played a pivotal role in its decision to endorse the establishment of a Scottish parliament with legislative powers in 1969, much to the chagrin of some prominent Labour cadres. The STUC recommendation was seen, by some, as a turning point in the long road to Scottish devolution that ended with the establishment of the Scottish Parliament at Holyrood in Edinburgh in 1999.

A few days before the January by-election, which Alex Rowley subsequently won at a canter, a news package from Cowdenbeath ran on Scottish television. It opened with a segment on the area's left-wing history featuring a short clip of Willie Clarke on the night of his election victory in Ballingry in 1973. The Communist candidate looked tired, his tie askew, his face puffy and red. He seemed older than his 37 years. But he smiled and received the interviewer's congratulations on his unexpected victory over the Labour incumbent in the firm, bass-heavy voice that had by then already become a fixture at miners' rallies in Fife and beyond. Not long after the cameras finished rolling, Clarke left the count centre to call his family from a roadside payphone. As he walked along the dimly lit road towards Cowdenbeath the lights of pit shafts dotted across the horizon sparkled against the night sky.

'And the idea just hit me walking along the road: that is your moment of glory passed. Now it's the hard work.'

Two days after his election, the phone rang at Willie Clarke's house. 'There's been an accident.'

The voice on the other end told Clarke to come to the Seafield Colliery right away. A roof in a steeply inclined coalface beneath the Firth of Forth had collapsed. Five miners were dead. It took rescue workers a week to reach the last three bodies.

'I was at the pit 'til two o'clock in the morning. After I went to the personnel manager's office. There were five folders underneath his desk. All their details, wives, families, everything. That's when it struck me what happened. All young boys, 20 years old. So you was away up here' – Clarke lifted his right arm in the air, and the sleeve of his grey jumper fell away slightly to reveal a thin, bright blue scar caused by trapped coal dust in a five-decade-old wound – 'and then bang. You were back to reality.'

In 1973, the National Union of Mineworkers (NUM) declared a work-to-rule in protest at the Conservative government's policy of public sector pay restraints amid spiralling inflation. Britain's coal stocks began to dwindle. That October, the oil crisis drove up the price of coal still further. Prime Minister Ted Heath, having failed to do a deal with the NUM, introduced the Three-Day Week in an effort to conserve fuel stocks. The United Kingdom, which less than 30 years earlier had won a war and ruled an empire on which the sun never set, appeared to many to be on the brink of collapse. On 23 December 1973, Tony Benn wrote in his diary: 'Three more IRA bombs in London. I tidied the office and wrapped Christmas gifts.'

Early in 1974, the NUM called a strike. Heath responded by

announcing a snap general election. The result was a hung parliament. The Scottish National Party, which had never won a seat in a general election before 1970, took seven seats. In fresh elections that October, the SNP increased its representation to 11. The nationalists' slogan – 'It's Scotland's Oil' – attempted to capture a sense that North Sea oil and gas could fuel independence. By that stage most of the mines in Fife had already closed.

* * *

Coal mining in Fife dates back at least as far as the 13th century, when monks were given a charter to dig for the 'black stanes that burned'. In the early years of the 19th century rich deposits of coal were inadvertently discovered at Cowdenbeath when iron ore shafts were sunk. Technology initially developed for extracting iron ore could be used to reach such deep coal seams. (Previously, only coal on the earth's surface had been accessible, through opencast mining.) Almost overnight Cowdenbeath, a tranquil cluster of farmers' cottages, was transformed into a noisy, dirty, ramshackle settlement. By the turn of the 20th century, the town's population had swelled to 14,000, many of them immigrants from Ireland and incomers from the established pit towns of Lanarkshire. The Fife Coal Company, Britain's largest mining enterprise, employed three quarters of the menfolk. If you lost your job, you lost your home.

As industrialisation took hold, so too did class politics. Trade unions were founded, as were more militant political vehicles. Among the latter was the UK branch of the Anarchist Communist League, initiated in 1908 in Cowdenbeath by Lawrence Storione, a French-Italian radical and pit worker. (Storione reputedly escaped persecution in France for his political beliefs by dressing as a woman and fleeing to Scotland. In Cowdenbeath, he married a local woman and bestowed on his children some wonderfully extravagant first names: Anarchie, Autonomie, Germinal and Libertie.) 'Our main slogan was "Trade Unions are bulwarks of capitalism and all Trade Union leaders are fakirs"' one of Storione's early disciples in Fife,

Bob Selkirk, recalled rather wistfully in a 1967 pamphlet entitled 'The Life of a Worker'.

In the spring of 1921, Cowdenbeath miners rejected a proposed 25 per cent wage cut. The Fife Coal Company responded by locking them out, using colliery officials to keep the pits going. There were skirmishes between protesters and police.

'After one clash and baton charges in Cowdenbeath, the strikers retaliated by breaking nearly all the shop windows in the High Street and helping themselves to the necessities stocked in the shop window,' recalled Bob Selkirk. The Cabinet in Westminster called in the army to guard the pitheads and arrest insurgents. As one elderly Communist told me, 'they thought the revolution would start here in Cowdenbeath'.

Before we went to the Benarty polling station that by-election morning, Willie Clarke brought me on a tour of the pit villages in his grey Renault Clio. On a nondescript kink in the road between Ballingry and Lochgelly he braked sharply, causing the papers scattered all over the back seat to fall onto the floor. A black briefcase almost followed.

'This was north Glencraig,' he announced. In front of us was a smooth, green field. A few saplings stood by the verges.

'To your right about 200 yards down the road, that was the colliery.' It was another green field, a little bumpier. I tried to imagine 1,500 men, their faces black with soot, walking back from here to their homes every day. I couldn't.

Willie Clarke was born in Glencraig in June 1935. His mother was a young, unmarried domestic servant when she became pregnant. In school, classmates would tease, 'Who is your father?'

Clarke lived with his mother and his uncle, who was a miner. The house, like many in Glencraig, had a subscription to the *Daily Worker*. His uncle used to take him to watch Raith Rovers play football in nearby Kirkcaldy on Saturday afternoons. During the war he collected short paperback biographies of all the Russian generals and pinned up two maps of Europe on the wall so that he and his nephew could mark the progress of the Allied and Axis forces as they followed radio reports from the front. (In January 1941, the *Daily Worker*, which took the Soviet Union line, was banned for undermining the war effort. The ban was lifted the following year, after the USSR had joined the Allied side.) In December 1947, Clarke's uncle died of a blood clot. He was just 39.

'It was just like a father died,' he recalled more than six and a half decades later.

At 14, Willie Clarke started work in the mine. His first job was separating stone from coal on the surface. He was paid less than 40 pence a shift. While most of the pit villages were solidly Labour, Glencraig was 'very militant'. Active Communists included Laurence Daly, a prominent miners' leader who would leave the Communist Party in 1956 in protest at Khrushchev's denunciation of Stalin. As we sat by the side of the road, I asked Clarke why he had become a communist. He thought for a moment.

'It caught your imagination, they were radical, wanted change, they were not prepared to accept things as they were.'

Over a number of years in the 1950s, Glencraig was demolished, the village's poorly built, overcrowded houses with their outdoor toilets having been deemed unfit for human habitation. Clarke and his mother, like most of their neighbours, were moved to a newly built house a few miles east, in Ballingry. The coal industry, nationalised in 1947, seemed as steadfast and dependable as the hard Fife ground on which it had been founded. In 1957, Prime Minister Harold Macmillan told Britain that 'most of our people have never had it so good.' That same year the Queen travelled to the Fife new town of Glenrothes to open a new colliery. Progress would march on, unabated. Living standards would continue to improve. But, subcutaneously, a different story was starting to unfold.

The Glenrothes colliery was a failure, and by the time it shut the following decade, mines across Scotland were being closed. The National Coal Board cited lack of productivity and exhausted seams in a 1962 report that recommended shifting production to a smaller number of high-volume sites and shedding 24,000 jobs in the industry. In October 1962, Harold Macmillan told his Cabinet that 'it was out of the question to allow Scotland or the Northeast, or any large area, to be abandoned to decay'. But the 'remedy did not lie in trying to preserve each individual community which had grown up for reasons long since irrelevant to modern conditions'. Reconciling these opposites, unsurprisingly, proved beyond Macmillan. Instead the discovery of much larger deposits of oil and gas than previously estimated in the North Sea hastened the demise of smaller mines across Britain. The most iconic in Cowdenbeath, No 7, with its unrivalled view from the pithead of Central Park, home of the 'Blue Brazil', Cowdenbeath FC, closed in 1960. Glencraig followed in 1966. The last deep mine in Scotland, Longannet in Fife, was closed in 2002.

Miners' leaders struggled to adjust to the new reality. Some reactionary union bosses, bloated with power, seemed almost oblivious of the situation facing ordinary workers; others called for radical action. In West Fife, this ideological distinction often took the form of tensions between Labour and Communists. Even in the 1970s, when all the local mines were gone and the area was clearly in need of alternative economic strategies, the two parties were at loggerheads in a political turf war.

'The local hatred was unbelievable, unbelievable,' Willie Clarke told me after we had finished our drive in Ballingry. The Communists often accused Labour of smear tactics, sometimes with good reason. And while individual members of both parties often got on well, publicly relations were bitter. The story sounded familiar, redolent of the acrimony between Labour and the SNP that characterises contemporary electoral politics in vast swathes of central Scotland and beyond.

Willie Clarke and I sat on plastic chairs in the small café in the corner of the Benarty Community Centre. The air was thick with the smell of soup and baby food. At the table opposite young mothers cradled infants. The centre is, in part, a testimony to the ageing communist's political effectiveness despite no longer having a party to support him. A state-of-the-art facility combining everything from the local police station and doctor's surgery to a library and a crèche under one roof, the Benarty Centre was opened in 2012 to replace a series of diffuse, dilapidated facilities dotted across the adjacent pit villages. A few years earlier, Clarke had successfully convinced the Scottish Nationalist administration in Edinburgh that the project would require £1.8 million in addition to the £2 million pledged by the previous Labour government. He holds his weekly constituency surgeries here, and as we sat chatting he exchanged a seemingly endless stream of smiling nods and greetings ('How are you, Ann?' 'See you at the meeting tomorrow, Mikey').

Just as Clarke was finishing a lunch of green pea soup and white bread slathered with butter, a mobility scooter silently edged up to our table. An elderly woman in a heavy coat said that her front door was so stiff she could barely open it. Clarke nodded. He took out a scrap of paper and a small, stubby bookmaker's pen. (He likes a bet on the horses, his friends told me.) He wrote down all the details. Across the hall, a photocopied sign was pinned up against a door: 'Benarty Heritage Preservation Group – the present preserving the past for the future'. Through the glass I could see a group of around a dozen mainly middle-aged men sitting around a table talking intently. One of them wore a black-and-white Dunfermline Athletic jersey. 'SCOT' was tattooed on the knuckles of one hand, 'LAND' on the other. A few minutes later, a tall man with straggly long hair and battered glasses approached.

'I've applied for that job you told me about up at Crosshill. Got an interview.'

Clarke smiled. 'Good, good.'

Later Clarke would take me to 'the Meedies', a picturesque lakeside park built on what was the former dump for the pits. The Meedies was once the largest land reclamation scheme in Europe. Now it is Fife's most popular tourist attraction. A group of teenagers on mountain bikes cycled across what had been a rail line for coal wagons. The white wooden frame of the old pit shaft peeked out behind a smattering of trees and brambles. When the park was built many locals wanted all traces of the mines removed. Willie Clarke was among those who successfully lobbied for the shaft to remain: 'Now if you tried to take it away there'd be a revolution.'

* * *

At its best, socialism is a prophetic, passionate, generous creed, which brings longed-for justice for many people. But in its utopian varieties, it has a major flaw.

It does not believe in sin.

RON FERGUSON (Rev.), *Black Diamonds and the Blue Brazil: A Chronicle of Coal, Cowdenbeath and Football*, 1993

In his book *The Country Formerly Known as Great Britain*, Ian Jack recalls that a relative who worked in a Cowdenbeath butcher's 'used to marvel at how much steak he sold to miners' wives on a Saturday'. There was both the cash and the organisation to sustain massive subscription drives that funded everything from Miner's Welfare Institutes and churches to parades and parks. Now, Cowdenbeath High Street is pockmarked with empty units and 'To Let' signs. Deindustrialisation has taken a heavy toll on a once vibrant, self-sufficient community. Jobs are scarce. In 2013, unemployment ran at over 15 per cent, the fourth highest rate in Scotland. The incidence of drug-related deaths is among the highest in the country.

Further along the High Street, an elderly man smoked outside the red sandstone council offices. In the 1920s, the town's Labour administration flew the Red Flag from the clock tower on the anniversary of the Russian Revolution. Nearby, a mobility scooter and a vacuum cleaner occupied the front window of 'Ideal Computers'. I went for lunch in the only café I could find with indoor seating. A thin, middle-aged man with an apron, a moustache and a stud in his ear smiled when I opened the door. He was standing in the middle of a linoleum-covered floor talking with three men seated at the only occupied table. They were Labour Party activists from the West of Scotland, in Cowdenbeath to help get the by-election vote out.

'Is that the voting over then?' the owner asked as he walked back to the counter.

'No, it'll go on until 10 tonight,' said the oldest of the group, a barrel-chested man with red cheeks.

'I'll be long gone by then though,' he added.

The two younger men seated by his side smiled. Both wore Labour pins on their jackets.

A little later, I went for an afternoon drink in a bar called the New Goth, which sits further down the High Street, in a dip just past the railway bridge. Outside, a sheet of A4 paper warned drinkers against smoking in the bar's entrance. The homemade sign was recent but the pub's blacked-out windows date back to its foundation in 1901. The New Goth was established according to the 'Gothenburg System', a Swedish approach to curbing excessive drinking amongst industrial workers. 'Goth' bars had austere interiors to discourage sessions. Spirits and games were proscribed. The bars were co-operatives. Shareholders pledged to take a dividend of no greater than five per cent. Any excess was reinvested into the community through improvements such as bowling greens and streetlights. The Gothenburg system was exported to Fife around the time that the docks were built at Methil to ease the passage of thousands of tonnes of coal to new markets in Scandinavia. When the first Goth pub was opened in Fife, in Kelty, *The Dundee Courier* said that it must be:

> regarded with the liveliest interest by all who wish to see a satisfactory settlement of one of the most vexed social questions of modern times.

The Goth concept spread across Scotland's mining villages. Almost all these pubs are closed now; or, like the New Goth, survive in name only.

The ascetic ethos of the original Goths would have appealed to many Fife Communists. Willie Gallacher was a lifelong teetotaller (as a teenager, the future MP left the temperance movement in disgust when he discovered that the director of a public house trust had been approached for campaign funds). Willie Sharp, the first Communist provost in Britain when he was elected in Cowdenbeath in 1973, did not smoke or drink. Communists decried religion 'as the opium of the people' (and were themselves denounced from the pulpits), but party and church often operated along similar lines. Both organised community events and Sunday Schools – one teaching the Bible, the other political economy and the works of Marx.

In late spring, I took the train to Cowdenbeath to meet Jackie Allan, one of the few remaining communist stalwarts in the town. Allan has a methodical manner, solemn yet welcoming, with a sharp face that gives way to soft brown eyes. He sat beside a small pile of books and a handful of meticulously scripted foolscaps on local communist history. He had underlined key dates. 1921, 1926, 1973, and 1984. Jackie Allan lives alone. His wife died four years earlier. On the wall were photos of her, their children and their grandchildren. Allan made tea and handed out miniature Kit-Kats, although he did not take one himself. Across the kitchen table sat Willie Clarke. For almost three hours the two men talked, about the situation in Ukraine and the Labour Party, about Margaret Thatcher and Scottish independence. But the subject they returned to most frequently was their mutual friend Alex Maxwell, who was initially elected as a Communist councillor in Cowdenbeath along with Willie Clarke in 1973. Maxwell stepped down in 2012 and died the following year.

'Again, non-smoker, non-drinker, strict disciplinarian, strong Communist,' said Clarke.

'Oh, he had discipline,' Jackie Allan agreed.

'No question, communists tended to be disciplined.'

'That's right, that's right.'

'If you wanted to organise something it had to be done right.'

Jackie's well-kept terraced house is on Selkirk Avenue. The street was named in honour of another councillor, Bob Selkirk, who, after his anarchist beginnings, became a leading communist in Cowden-

Little Moscow, Lumphinnans

beath. A mile or so down the road, at Lumphinnans, women hung washing outside two-storey houses on Gallacher Place and Gagarin Way. This area is known as 'Little Moscow', another throwback to the Communist past.

'I'm the only one left who is active,' Jackie Allan said after the tea was finished. 'You have Communist-minded boys here but I'm really the only one left. The Selkirks are away and the Maxwells, that was a big blow to me, I have to say. I am the only one who is left.' Allan was a firm yes voter. 'But Willie is the one who is really involved in the (referendum) campaign.' As he spoke Jackie Allan slowly ran the foolscap sheets back and forth between his fingers.

* * *

Early on the evening of 9 November 1989, Günter Schabowski, First Secretary of the East Berlin branch of the Socialist Unity Party of Germany, was about to address his daily press conference when he was handed a note. The previous months had seen escalating protests on the streets of the city. The East German Politburo had decided to announce new travel regulations, allowing anyone who wanted to go to West Germany to do so through East Germany's border crossings with official permission. The new arrangements were supposed to come into force the following day, but nobody had explained the specifics of the changes to Schabowski. Asked by a reporter when they would come into effect, the East Berlin Communist Party boss replied haltingly, 'As far as I know – immediately, without delay.' Tens of thousands of East Berliners flocked to the wall. Within a matter of hours, the barricade that separated East and West for almost 30 years was effectively gone. The Communist regimes of Eastern Europe, and then the Soviet Union itself, would follow in short order.

In Cowdenbeath, Mary Doherty, who organised the Socialist Sunday School, burst out crying when she saw the images from Berlin on the evening news. They were not tears of joy.

'Her world was shattered,' recalled Jackie Allan. 'Everything was the Soviet Union, you had a vision. What kept me going personally was that vision, that was the vision you reached for. Then it was gone.'

Alex Maxwell, once the subject of a flattering pen portrait in *Pravda*, said that the fall of the Berlin Wall was 'like telling a Christian there was no God'.

The Communist Party of Great Britain was in terminal decline long before the Wall fell. Tensions between pro-Soviet voices and 'Eurocommunists' deepened during the 1970s. In 1977 a cadre of hardliners broke away to form the New Communist Party of Britain. Just over a decade later, another group of anti-revisionists that had coalesced around a network of *Morning Star* readers' groups founded the Communist Party of Britain. These schisms had limited impact on the Communists in West Fife, who broadly maintained their support for the original party. In Scotland, Communists continued to play an important – if often unacknowledged – role in the campaign for a devolved parliament, especially after Thatcher's third successive election victory in 1987. But by the early 1990s, the entire communist edifice in the East had collapsed. With its lodestar, the Soviet Union, gone, the Communist Party of Great Britain voted to disband itself in 1991. The think tank Democratic Left was established in its place. In Scotland, around 280 Communists, including miners' leader Mick McGahey, founded the Communist Party of Scotland.

This was, Willie Clarke said with characteristic understatement, a 'difficult period'. Alex Maxwell joined Democratic Left. Willie Clarke threw his hat in with the Scottish Communists, becoming chairman in the 1990s before eventually leaving as the party's limited support ebbed away. Recently I walked past a stall festooned with Communist Party flags on a busy Saturday on Buchanan Street, Glasgow's pedestrianised main shopping thoroughfare. Half a dozen hirsute men, mostly of retirement age, were trying to sell newspapers. The passing public showed little interest. The 'Discover Islam' gazebo on the opposite side of the street was enjoying much more success.

Willie Clarke still describes himself as a communist. He is an independent but he campaigns on an avowedly communistic platform. 'All the (election) literature that goes out is communist,' he said.

'My name, my photograph, communist. Everything that goes out, so nobody can say you're trying to gild the lily. I'm still a communist.'

On our second meeting I asked Clarke if he remembered the day, in 1968, when the Warsaw Pact forces crushed the Prague Spring. He told me he was coming up from a day shift in the colliery when the news broke.

'A boy, Peter Clarke, no relation, he was the engineer, shouted to me, "Willie, they've sent troops into Czechoslovakia." And I thought to myself, "Jesus, how stupid can you be. What are you playing at."' The invasion left 72 Czechoslovakians dead. The party hierarchy in Britain dismissed it as an 'intervention'. Clarke said he was 'shocked' by the Soviet forces' vicious reprisals but he did not quit the party.

Between the early 1960s and the late 1980s, Clarke visited China and the Soviet Union a number of times. He speaks fondly of weeks spent in Moscow at the height of the Cold War. Denunciations of the Soviet Union, he maintained, were motivated by anti-communism, not a desire to shed light on repression. 'There were attacks made on the Soviet Union all the time, but that was not because they wanted to change it, they just wanted to attack it.

We saw the Soviet Union as the vanguard of the working classes of the whole world.'

When Willie was elected in 1973 some of his party colleagues were publicly supportive of the Soviet Union yet privately well aware of the brutal reality of life for many in communist Russia. The Soviet Union, Clarke said, had 'made mistakes' but he felt at the time that it needed to be supported. It was only after the wall fell that he, and the rest of the world, realised the full extent of the brutality of the regime in Russia and across Eastern Europe.

'What you believed was happening in the Soviet Union wasn't happening at all,' he said, referring to the Soviet propaganda that regularly featured in communist newspapers in the West, including *The Morning Star.*

When he was a teenager Jackie Allan asked his father why the family always voted Communist.

'His answer was simple: "They're the people who help you the most".' Willie Clarke's version of communism retains this hopeful, almost folksy air. He talks of communism as a higher calling that assumes the best of humanity. There are no secret police, show trials or gulags, just an appeal to man's better nature. Four decades on from his first election victory, the material conditions that sustained Fife's pit villages – and its communists – are gone. The mines are closed, and Willie Clarke is able to win votes not because of his belief in a new socialist order but because he works tirelessly to get council houses renovated and community centres opened.

Scottish politics has changed, too. Not only are the Communists an electoral irrelevance in Scotland but so too, largely, is the Conservative Party. The battle is now an increasingly rancorous one between Labour and the SNP. The big question in Scottish politics for the foreseeable future is independence, not industrial policy.

During the referendum some of the loudest – and most coherent – voices for leaving the Union came from the Scottish Left. The youthful Radical Independence Campaign (RIC) played an active role in rallying working class voters in the housing schemes of central Scotland. RIC and its energised activists launched voter registration drives and held mass canvasses. Under banners that proclaimed 'Another Scotland is Possible', they criticised the SNP's centrist vision of a low-tax, social democratic independent Scotland and called for a return to class politics. Their tactics seemed to resonate: working-class voters were the group that said Yes in the greatest numbers on 18 September. It was not enough to swing the referendum, but these activists hope that they have created a solid base from which a left wing movement can develop. In November 2014, the RIC held their annual conference at the SECC auditorium on the banks of the Clyde in Glasgow. All 3,000 tickets were sold out weeks in advance.

In 2013, the Scottish Left Review Press published a collection of essays, *Scotland's Road to Socialism*. The title was a knowing echo of the Communist Party of Great Britain's post-war programme *The British Road to Socialism*. The Communist Party of Great Britain, however, was opposed to independence. During the referendum campaign the party's Scottish Committee called for a No vote as a 'springboard for remobilising the working class movement at the British level to demand real constitutional change'.

'I couldn't believe that,' said Jackie Allan as he sat at his kitchen table on Selkirk Avenue reflecting on the position taken by some of his former comrades.

Willie Clarke shook his head. 'If we were talking about Communists around here I'd say they're all for independence.'

For months leading up to the referendum, Willie Clarke was one of the moving spirits in the Benarty branch of the Yes Scotland campaign. His son, also Willie, and his grandson were both members, too. Most weeks, crowds in their hundreds packed into the Benarty centre to watch speakers including Dennis Canavan, chair of the Yes Scotland advisory board, and Colin Fox, leader of the pro-independence Scottish Socialist Party.

'I never saw a campaign like it in my life,' Willie Clarke said as we drove through Lochgelly the afternoon before the referendum. Smiling, he pointed out every single Yes flag and banner that lined the road. There were dozens. Willie Clarke looked happier than I'd ever seen him.

* * *

Around lunchtime on 17 September, a bagpiper heralded the arrival of Gordon Brown at a community hall in Glasgow. Once the music faded out, the former Prime Minister launched into a speech that by the end of the day was being hailed by some over zealous scribes as the oration 'that saved the Union'. A little over a week earlier Brown had effectively bounced the Westminster leadership into making a pledge for more powers for Holyrood in a speech at the Loanhead Miners Welfare and Social Club in Midlothian. Now, clearly fired up by his return to frontline politics, the erstwhile Labour leader called on supporters 'to stand up and be counted'. His words would lead news bulletins that night.

As crowds waving 'No Thanks' placards applauded Gordon Brown in Glasgow, I was sitting 60 miles away in a backroom at the Benarty centre with Willie Clarke and Michael Payne, an education worker in the centre. It was my first visit in a couple of months. The café had closed. Business had been bad and there was not enough cash running through the till to cover staffing costs. Neither man was exactly confident of victory but they were more hopeful than earlier in the summer.

'I've not seen anything like this in terms of public meetings. The last time I saw this community galvanised like this was the miner's strike,' said Payne, a bright-eyed Celtic supporter with soft red hair. 'The solidarity is still there. It died a bit after the miner's strike but it's back now.'

Just after 6.00am on Friday morning, 'the Kingdom of Fife' declared: 55.05 per cent No, 44.95 per cent Yes. The result almost exactly mirrored the national outcome, and spelt the end for any lingering hopes among independence supporters. Scotland would definitely be staying in the Union. As the returning officer solemnly announced the outcome, I thought of Willie Clarke driving me back to Cowdenbeath train station 36 hours earlier.

'I believe that Scotland will be an independent nation,' he had said, looking straight ahead. 'If it doesn't happen now it'll be happen in the future. Maybe I'll not see it but it'll happen.'

In the days immediately after the vote there was disillusionment among independence activists in Ballingry and Lochgelly. Many had expected a win, making defeat even more difficult to stomach. There was anger, and sadness too. Then something strange happened. The Yes meetings started up again. There were discussions about what powers the Smith Commission could deliver for the devolved parliament and whether a cross-party Yes Alliance should run on a pro-independence ticket in the 2015 general election. In November, two months after the vote, a Yes gathering in Kirkcaldy attracted over 250 people.

'I said that the referendum was only the start of something but I never thought it would be this,' Willie Clarke said. 'It's incredible.' It was early November and his voice sounded lighter, more hopeful than on the eve of the referendum. With so much political activity going on around him, would he be standing again as a councillor, I asked, a little mischievously. He laughed. He had not decided. The next election was almost three years away. A political lifetime. 'But whether I was a councillor or not I'd still be involved in politics. No question. Activists never retire.'

CHAPTER THREE

The Debatable Lands

WHEN I WAS a teenager my parents decided it would be a good idea to take a weeklong family holiday in Scotland. My father drove our wine-coloured Peugeot 405 to Belfast, where we caught the ferry to Stranraer. The crossing was choppy. We sloshed around in the bar surrounded by middle-aged men with thick moustaches and bristling Belfast accents. As we docked in Scotland the hirsute drinkers clambered on to a bus with a piece of paper that said 'Glasgow' tacked onto the front window. Our family gingerly climbed back into the car and drove an hour-or-so to our first destination, Dumfries.

My memories of that visit to Dumfries are hazy. We spent a couple of days schlepping around houses that claimed some connection with Robert Burns. At night we stayed in a hotel with peeling wallpaper that sat off a pedestrianised street in the centre of town. Once or twice I escaped the room I shared with my younger brother, going down a side street between our hotel to cough on a surreptitious cigarette. I wanted to try all the different brands I could not get back home: Lambert and Butler; Royal Crowns; Benson and Hedges Sovereign. To a 14-year-old from a small Irish town the names spoke of an exotic, imperial age.

I mention all this because it was almost 20 years later, about a month before the referendum, that I returned to Dumfries for the first time. The town, the largest in Dumfries and Galloway, seemed surprisingly familiar. The rows of well-appointed houses and once grand municipal buildings hewn out of red sandstone looked solidly impressive, unflappable in the inevitable rain that drifted in from the Solway Firth. A strident Burns in white marble sat atop a plinth, facing a reasonably busy High Street. The Our Price store where my teenage self had bought the Super Furry Animals' first album on cassette was gone. (I think the store was in Dumfries, but it could have been Perth. We stayed in a lot of medium-sized Scottish towns on that holiday.) Two decades on shoppers carrying plastic bags trooped up and down the street in the early afternoon drizzle. Around the corner, a well-dressed couple walked purposefully into a Barbour concession.

All Dumfries was not stolid prosperity, however. Across from the colonnades of the Procurator Fiscal's office a group of teenage girls huddled in the doorway of a youth centre. A little further down the street, towards the bridge that spanned the River Nith, a sign in the window of what looked like an abandoned accountants' office said 'Food Donations Urgently Required'. Below the text was a drawing of a loaf of bread and a handful of overlapping sheaves of wheat. I had reached my destination, the First Base Agency, a Dumfries-based charity that runs a food bank and a shelter for those in need. I pushed open the door. The air inside was warm and clammy. Boxes of cereal were stacked high against a bookcase. A notice on the wall warned that 'solvent abuse kills'. A man with long, greasy hair and tattoos on his arms disappeared out of view up a flight of stairs behind the reception.

'We have gone from 100 to 500 food parcels a month purely on the back of the welfare reforms from Westminster,' Mark Frankland, director of First Base said as we sat in a wood-panelled annex beyond the reception.

Frankland filled a green armchair, his large hands cradling a cup of instant coffee. The room had, at various times in the past, been a bakery, a café and a craft shop. Vestiges of its previous incarnations remained in the colourful glass bottles that lined the window and the hanging plants that hugged the wall. The place had a Scandinavian feel, a consciously 'safe space' created for those unfortunate souls for whom havens are as fleeting as they are vital. A booklet entitled *Living with a Child Coming Off Drugs* sat on the coffee table. A nearby coaster warned 'Keep Your Eyes on Your Drink'.

Frankland had the air of an inspirational teacher, or perhaps even a preacher. He had unkempt, wiry hair, thinning at the temples and looked out from behind black-rimmed glasses. He was passionate, speaking in long, sonorous sentences about the social injustices he saw all around him. On his jacket was a bright red badge: Yes. Earlier, the young receptionist had described herself as 'a definite Yes'. She looked past me at a pile of boxes, as if to say that the food parcels inside explained her voting intention.

Dumfries

'A lot of folks we meet here live on the schemes. Life isn't great. They say everyone is voting Yes there,' Frankland said, tipping the ash off the end of a Camel Light. His was hardly a typical independence activist's story: born in Lancashire, Frankland had moved to Dumfries with his wife and two children in 1996. Seven years later he opened First Base after a chance encounter with a heroin addict in a local café. But, in some ways, Frankland was emblematic of the energised political neophytes that seemed to populate the edges of the Yes campaign in the months leading up to the referendum. He had begun blogging about independence, and then progressed to appearing alongside politicians at debates across Dumfries and Galloway and the Borders. The following evening he was due to appear at an event in a local pub alongside Tommy Sheridan. Many Yes campaigners had refused to share a stage with Sheridan, adopting a 'no platform' policy towards the former Scottish Socialist Party leader and convicted perjurer, but Frankland had become firm friends with Sheridan. His biggest concern was the paucity of undecided voters at the debates he spoke at.

'One of the things that has been slightly disappointing is that any meeting I've been speaking at it's been 80 per cent Yes,' Frankland said, stubbing out another cigarette.

Throughout the referendum campaign I was continually surprised by the range of answers elicited by the question 'why do you want independence?' For Mark Frankland leaving the Union was necessary to deliver a written constitution and a bill of rights. He had, he said, seen authoritarian states first-hand travelling in Eastern Europe and the Middle East in the 1980s and 90s. His concerns about civil liberties regularly featured in the thrillers he wrote with impressive alacrity.

'How many books have you written?' I asked at one stage.

'Oh, about 18.'

A copy of one, *Mere Anarchy,* looked down from a shelf in the consulting room. The cover was a skeleton in what appeared to be the uniform of a Nazi infantryman framed by a blood red sky. He had written a book about a Palestinian refugee family in Glasgow and another, *The Cull,* about drug abuse in Dumfries. (The area has a long-standing smack problem. Earlier in 2014, police seized heroin worth £1.2m from a car on the M74 near Dumfries.) An Amazon reviewer commended Frankland's *Terrible Beauty,* set in Belfast during the Troubles, for its verisimilitude:

> The author has taken a heavy subject and written a page turner, having read it again, I still couldn't put it down.

Frankland was 'hugely confident' of victory in the referendum, predicting a 60/40 vote for Yes. And what about Dumfries and the Scottish Borders, renowned bastions of Unionist sentiment?

'It'll be 50/50 here, which means we'll win everywhere else.

I asked how he would feel if it was a No. He grimaced. 'I'd be sick as a parrot.'

Throughout the campaign he had been publishing a new book, *Toxic,* chapter-by-chapter online. 'It's like Dickens did,' he smiled. *Toxic* was set against the backdrop of the referendum. The final instalment appeared on 18 September. The closing lines were less hopeful than their author had been a few weeks earlier: 'And then they climbed back on board their quad bikes and left the old glacial rocks in the clearing to another million years of silence.'

* * *

Everyone admits the Border countryside is of another world, of a
limpid beauty, tranquillity and gentle intensity that stuns if only
because the visible gawping tourists are almost nil.

JOHN MURRAY, *Reiver Blues*, 1996

Borders are defining lines, creating places and people, nations and
nationalities. The border between England and Scotland is one of
the world's oldest, and the line that separates the two countries is
often envisaged as a straight one running east to west. Perhaps the
erroneous journalistic shorthand for Scotland 'north of Hadrian's
Wall' is at least partly responsible for this fallacy. If anything, the
meandering border stretches broadly north to south, from its most
easterly point beyond Berwick's town limits to Gretna, 80 miles or
so southwest.

The Scottish Borders is often depicted as a peaceful land of picturesque villages, panoramic valleys and horizon-filling peat bog. Conservative, with a small 'c' and a large one. The Borders were expected
to deliver a solid No on September 18, just as they had done in the
ill-fated 1979 devolution referendum. Then as now, why change
what does not need changing is a common sentiment in well-to-do
Borders' towns and villages.

But the border between England and Scotland was not always
so tranquil. Between the 13th and the 16th centuries the Borders
was a wild, dangerous place. During the violent, intermittent wars
between England and Scotland, Godfrey Watson wrote, Borderers
could 'rarely go to sleep without the fear of attack'. Often the
assault came not from armies of one kingdom or another, but from
Border 'Reivers', the rough balladeering men who launched frequent
raids into enemy territory, stealing livestock and disrupting quotidian
life. Nonetheless, in the same partisan manoeuvring seen today across
borders from Kosovo to South Sudan, trouble at the frontier often
served a political purpose for the Scottish and English potentates.

Although Scotland and England were frequently at war, the

border was legally established in 1237. The frontier counties were divided into three districts, or, 'Marches' on each side: the East March took in Berwick and its environs on the Scottish side, North-east Northumberland and parts of the Palatinate of Durham in England; the Middle March extended as far north as the Scottish town of Peebles and to the south took in the rest of Northumberland and districts including Tynedale and Redesdale; the West March encompassed Dumfries as well as Cumberland and Westmorland. There was, however, a geographical black spot, what Watson calls 'the only blot on an otherwise tidy arrangement for administering the Border': 'The Debatable Lands'.

The Debatable Lands, as the name suggests, were held by neither Scotland nor England but claimed by both. Local clans controlled the territory, about 40 square miles all told extending from the Solway Firth at Gretna to Langholm in Dumfries and Galloway. The names of the clansmen have a familiar ring: Armstrong, Elliot, Scott, Charlton, Robson, Bell, Graham. These are the surnames of many of the largest landowners on both sides of the Borders today. Four centuries ago these were the families that, backed by a clan-based devotion to banditry and romantic notions of honour, marshalled some of the most ferocious of the Reivers. The lawless Debatable Lands helped ensure that order was hard to maintain across the Border Marches. In 1518, for example, Lord Dacre arrested 'ten of the principal thieves among the highlandmen of Redesdale'. The prisoners were dispatched to Rothbury under an 80-strong guard. Redesdale Reivers, however, slipped across the moors and ambushed the party en route, killing the bailiff and six of his men, before disappearing over the border into Scotland. As the 1520s wore on, the Border Reviers became increasingly notorious. In Scotland, they were cursed by the national churches and even excommunicated. English Reviers (who were often related to their Scottish foes) suffered a similar fate. But business was good; the thievery continued.

The Reivers, however, were starting to outlive their political utility. Henry VIII even wrote to his royal cousin of Scotland suggesting that the Borders be 'planted' with a new population, presumably along the lines of what was soon to transpire in Ireland. That plan came to nought. Instead what eventually sealed the Reivers' fate was the same event that spelled the end of an independent Scotland: the Union of the Crowns. On 25 March 1603, the realms of Scotland, England and Ireland came under the control of a single monarch, James VI – who, confusingly, became James I of England and Ireland in the process. Overnight, the strategic rationale for allowing the Reivers to run amok vanished. The rampaging Border men were living on borrowed time.

James moved quickly. He changed the name of the Border counties to the Middle Shires, in an effort to inculcate a newfound sense of unity between the once bellicose kingdoms. He then set about destroying the Reivers and the conditions that allowed them to thrive. The Debatable Lands in the early years of the 17th century must have felt like the last days of the Wild West. Reivers were rounded up by the dozen. Strongholds on both sides of the border were demolished: 30 or 40 towers belonging to the Elliots alone were razed to the ground. The ordinary law of the land replaced the cruder Borders variant. From now on the theft of good or cattle 'amounting to the value of 12d' was punishable by death. There are reports of broken men being hung in Hawick until the town ran out of rope. In September 1606, Sir George Home, charged with pacifying both counties, reported having cause to 'hang 140 of the nimblest and most powerful thieves in all the Borders'. Some of the most notorious clansmen, including the Bold Buccleuch, became instruments for the new dispensation, assisting in the capture of former allies. Such role reversals should not be surprising. Class has almost always been more important than nationality among the Scottish aristocracy. The prevailing lack of concern shown by many lairds towards their compatriots during the Highland Clearances was hardly a one-off.

Mollifying the Borders took time. In 1611, 92 Reivers were brought to trial. Thirty-eight were executed at Jedburgh and Dumfries. The Debatable Lands themselves were viewed as almost beyond redemption on account of the villainy that the boggy hills and shallow valleys had played host to for much of the preceding centuries. Commissioners talked of removing the inhabitants to a place 'where the change of air will make in them an exchange of their manners'. Many prominent families were transferred to the bogs of Connaught where they were expected to cultivate the sodden soil for local landlords. Others were sent to fight in battles from Bohemia to Ireland. Many found God: the Borders became a fastness of religion. The Covenanters later flourished in the soft border soil. Overtime the Borders were pacified. The belligerent reputation was replaced by a softer image of soporific bucolicism. The Borders, in the popular imaginary, became a place where change happened slowly, if it happened at all. The people voted Liberal or Conservative and displayed little appetite for radicalism. But it was not always thus.

* * *

'We're looking for the cairn.'

The woman behind the counter in the Cadbury's outlet store in the Gretna Gateway shopping centre stared silently over my shoulder. All around her, piled precariously high, were clear plastic bags filled to bursting with Roses chocolates and mini-Wispas. 'Any 2 for £6,' declared signs in red dotted across the shop.

'We're looking for the cairn,' I tried again. 'Rory Stewart's cairn.'

There was a flicker of recognition. 'Oh yeah, that.'

The directions were not great, but they were good enough. After wandering through the sprawling Gateway car park – past Ulster-

The Auld Acquaintance Cairn, Gretna

bus coaches half full of visitors clutching shopping bags with Tartan motifs – myself and my companion, a young bearded Green-tinged academic from Edinburgh, finally spotted a homemade sign on the edge of the road: 'The Cairn'. An arrow pointed into a field.

The 'Auld Acquaintances Cairn' was the brainchild of Rory Stewart. Stewart, the often-thoughtful former deputy governor in Iraq and current Conservative MP for Penrith and the Border, had opened the cairn a few months earlier, in July. The independence debate had, he said at the time, 'been too much about politicians and celebrities and not enough about giving ordinary people the chance to show how they feel.' Stewart's answer was a circular pile of rocks and scree beside a car park on the border. Behind it flags of all the nations in the union fluttered in the stiff breeze. Traffic whirred past on the road just beyond the hedge. It was very loud.

Stewart had hoped, he said, that the cairn would reach nine feet tall, but three weeks before the referendum it was barely a third of that. A short walkway connected the cairn's outer and inner walls. It looked more like a miniature golf course than an archaeological

The Auld Acquaintance Cairn

relic. We spent half an hour wandering around the site. There was nobody else there. The whole scene could have been borrowed from an episode of *Father Ted*. There was a gazebo in blue and white with Stewart's name above it and a pair of empty deck chairs. A sign invited visitors to add a fresh stone to the pile. ('If you are feeling strong spend 10 minutes taking handfuls of rocks to the cairn,' it suggested.) You could even paint your lump of rock. Open tins in shades of red, white and blue stood adjacent to a plastic bag filled with used gloves. On the ground, an orgy of spilt paint bore a passing resemblance to an A-level student's pastiche of Jasper Johns. Some of the rocks on the cairn carried popular unionist slogans. One said 'Better Together', another 'Let's Stay as One'. The menacing 'All One Blood All One Nation' was more the exception than the rule.

One particularly ornate slab of drystone, decorated with the Union flag and the Scottish Saltire, declared 'Proud to be Scottish. Proud to Be British. Please Let's Stay Together.' The 'Please' was underlined, as if to emphasis the essential politeness of it all. The cairn had all the reserve for which the Borders had become renowned in the centuries since the last Reiver hung up his cattle-rustling boots (or was hung up himself). Even the 'Yes to independence' scrawled in the cairn's well-thumbed guest book appeared more mischievous than malicious.

The Auld Acquaintances Cairn was meant to symbolise the connection between Scotland and England, to evoke the 'great' in Great Britain as David Cameron might have said. (That 'great' is itself a geographical appellation, like Greater Glasgow, not a description of the nation's prowess, but such semantics rarely bother politicians or their speechwriters.) As it was Rory Stewart's empty field with its hill of stones and half full tins of paint looked doleful, even pathetic. I found myself feeling sorry for the people who have taken the time to come to Gretna, to park their cars and carry their stones to an unloved hillock of rocks. Throughout the referendum, Better Together – dubbed 'Project Fear' on account of its oft-unrelenting negativity – spoke of economic uncertainty and 'the pound in your pocket', not of four nations united. Where was the heart in the Union? Where was the emotional case for why these four peoples really were better together? Scotland did eventually vote No, but if the Union is to survive another 30 years (never mind 300) these questions will continue to demand answers. Nations are, in Benedict Anderson's oft-repeated phrase, 'imagined communities', but they need stories that speak to the heart as well as the head to keep the collective disbelief suspended. To see those stories in Stewart's cairn perhaps required more belief than I could summon.

From Sark Bridge, overlooking the cairn, England spreads itself. The hills of Cumbria rise up in the distance. Just down the road, at Burgh Marsh, is a monument to King Edward I who died attempting to invade and conquer Scotland in 1307. The English got a measure of revenge in 1542 at Solway Moss, near what is now Gretna Junction, when they routed a Scottish army.

Before we left the cairn, my Greenie friend and I walked across a molehill-filled field to the River Sark. 'So this is the border?' I asked.

'I believe so, yeah.'

We stood staring in silence at an inert stretch of water, about ten feet wide. A rust-coloured leaf fell from an overhanging tree. It felt very peaceful.

* * *

> After journeying over most of Scotland, England and central, southern and eastern Europe, as well as America, Siberia, and China, I am of the opinion that 'my native place' – the Muckle Toon of Langholm, in Dumfriesshire – is the bonniest place I know...
>
> HUGH MacDIARMID, 'Growing Up in Langholm',
> in *Memoirs of a Modern Scotland*, 1970

Set in a valley a few miles inside the border and a 20 minute drive from Gretna, *the* Langholm is an attractive little town. Tree-lined hills look down on neat streets of brick houses and busy shops selling artisan chocolates and colourful tweed. The River Esk burbles along happily through the centre of town. Langholm feels less like the erstwhile Reiver fastness it once was, and more like the setting for an autumnal edition of *Songs of Praise*. There is a sleepy sense of permanence, epitomised by the town hall, an imposing, fortress-like quondam tollbooth that sits flush in the middle of the main street, forcing traffic to bend to its will and weave around it. Langholm sits on the edge of the constituency of Dumfriesshire, Clydesdale and Tweeddale. It was the only seat in Scotland to return a Conservative MP in the 2010 general election. In the run-up to the referendum, polls suggested some 97 per cent of Tory supporters intended to vote No.

For a small place, Langholm has many famous descendants: Neil Armstrong, first man on the moon and ruddy-faced recipient of the freedom of Langholm, as a plaque in the car park behind the town hall attests; US televangelist Billy Graham (another Reiver name); Thomas Telford, the architect and engineer who bequeathed Langholm £3,000 that could only be used to buy books; and, most recently, Christopher Murray Grieve, aka Hugh MacDiarmid, who lived for more than a decade in the town hall when it was the Post Office buildings and his father the local postmaster. The young Grieve spent countless hours in the second floor library erected to house Telford's munificence. MacDiarmid, easily the most controversial Scottish nationalist poet of his, or any other, generation later wrote in an essay entitled 'Growing Up in Langhom':

> Before I left home (when I was 14) I could go up into that library in the dark and find any book I wanted. I read almost every one of them.

The library is still there. On a soggy weekday morning, I stumbled up its dark stairs with current custodian Ron Addison.

'You've come to the right place at the right time,' Addison, an avuncular retiree with a degree in Scottish history, said as we reached a narrow landing. He flicked the light switch inside the door of the library. Overhead strip lights hummed into life. The room was small, with no windows, and was lined with thin carpet and shelf after shelf of books with such racy titles as *Practice and Procedure in the Church of Scotland* and *The Covenanters*. The entire back wall was a colourful display dedicated to MacDiarmid. There were photographs of a serious looking young poet, his striking hollow face framed by a Royal Army Medical Corp uniform, and of a craggy-faced Grieve in his dotage, reclining on an armchair surrounded by books in his home. There were framed copies of LPs of his readings, and a verse in honour of MacDiarmid by his friend, the 'Zen Calvinist' poet Norman MacCaig. When Ron Addison was at university, MacCaig had been his tutor.

Half the wall was given over to a map of Langholm. Drawing pins denoted sites associated with MacDiarmid. There was a mark at his birthplace in Arkingholm Terrace and another at Langholm cemetery, where the poet was buried. Further along the wall was a spartan black and white election poster. 'Vote Dr C. M. Grieve (Communist Candidate)'. In the accompanying headshot MacDiarmid wears a suit and tie, but his shock of grey hair and wild eyes give the game away. He was standing in the 1964 general election in Perth and Kinross, hardly a communist stronghold. Sir Alec Douglas Home took the seat for the Conservatives with a massive two-thirds of the vote. MacDiarmid polled just 127.

'He was a communist. The folks around here, the Duke of Buccleuch, they didn't like communists,' said Addison.

But MacDiarmid was more than just a communist – which is one of the main reasons his literary legacy remains so divisive. ('Fuck MacDiarmid', a writerly friend messaged me when I said I was off to Langholm.) In 1928, the poet was a founder member of the National Party of Scotland, forerunner of the SNP. Five years earlier, writing in the *Scottish Nation*, MacDiarmid had said that 'we need a Scottish Fascism'. How far, if at all, his tongue was inserted in his cheek is unclear; MacDiarmid's was an idealistic Celtic nationalism peppered with often overt anti-English sentiment. In a 1940 letter to the poet Sorley Maclean, MacDiarmid described the French and British bourgeoisie as a 'far greater enemy' than the

Nazis. Around this time he was among the loosest cannons in a less than watertight SNP. In the 1945 general election, MacDiarmid was selected, against opposition from the party hierarchy, to stand on a nationalist ticket in Glasgow Kelvingrove. During the course of the campaign MacDiarmid slandered his leader, Arthur Donaldson, and made anti-English remarks at an election meeting in Glasgow. He tried to explain away the latter, saying they were his personal views rather than SNP policy. MacDiarmid clearly had little regard for the niceties of party fealty. He was subsequently excluded from the party's National Council. Earlier, MacDiarmid had been expelled from the Communist Party for his personal attacks – the Scottish tradition of *flyting* – on former comrade and fellow writer Edwin Muir.

The shelves of the gloomy Langholm library housed some of Grieve's personal collection. There were stories by Eric Linklater and a heavy tome on Edwardian Scotland. Addison smiled as he pointed out a bound edition of Bret Harte, a 19th century journalist turned novelist with a name like a professional wrestler and a fondness for gamblers, rouges and colourful characters of the California gold rush era. (Andrew Carnegie was also a fan.) I imagined Harte's outlaw spirit left a deep imprint on the young MacDiarmid. There certainly seems little point in searching for political consistency – as some have done – in a man who wrote, as MacDiarmid did in *A Drunk Man Looks at the Thistle*, that he would always be where 'Extremes meet – it's the only way I ken'. What else but wilful obstinacy could explain the poet's decision to rejoin the Communist Party in 1957, at the very moment when writers and intellectuals were rushing for the exit in the wake of the invasion of Hungary? But should we really expect our writers, whether MacDiarmid or anyone else, to be cogent political voices, too? Probably not. Both sides in the referendum debate were less circumspect. Unionists trumpeted JK Rowling's backing so loudly that one could be forgiven for thinking Hogwarts was an electoral district. On the independence side, Janice Galloway, Irvine Welsh and a plethora of belle-lettrists all publicly called for a Yes vote.

Langholm appeared unmoved by these literary interjections into the political decisions of the day, just as it had been in MacDiarmid's. Ron Addison attributed the absence of Yes and No posters to 'people waiting to make up their minds.' Tom, another library volunteer who had arrived as I stood admiring the MacDiarmid montage, had a different take.

'We're suspicious of any outside administration. Carlisle is our closest centre but the mindset changes when you have to go to Carlisle. We are very conscious of our local identity.' Tom was dressed as if he was about to play a round of golf, in slacks and a large sweater. Unlike Ron Addison who had come from Edinburgh, Tom had spent his whole life in the Middle Shires. 'That's the way we are here,' he said, sighing lightly for effect, I fancied.

I left the library and took a short walk over the Esk, to a local arts centre named after the Duke of Buccleuch. The café was empty save two middle-aged English men and their Scottish wives who sat sipping mid-morning coffees. I introduced myself as a journalist.

'Oh, no we couldn't speak to you,' one of the ladies politely demurred. Her companions all nodded solemnly. A quarter of an hour later I was still sitting at their table talking about the referendum. They would not say how they were voting but it was not hard to guess.

'A lot of people here depend on things in England', said the older looking of the two men.

During the referendum campaign there had been dire warnings that independence would lead to restricted access to services in England for those on the Scottish side of the border or, more shrilly, that armed guards could be posted on border crossings. His friend was worried about the English being blamed if there was a narrow No.

'They'll say it's our fault'. He looked genuinely worried.

Back on the High Street, I called into one of the art galleries. (Langholm is the kind of town that has not one but a selection of galleries on its main street.) The bright walls were covered in impressionistic paintings of the verdant Borders countryside. The gallery's owner was a Yes voter from Stoke-on-Trent.

'As an English person living in Scotland I've got no axe to grind. I just think that [independence] would be great thing for Scotland.' He seemed to be one of the few in Langholm.

On the road out of Langholm, towards Hawick, I swung a hard right at a sign for the Hugh MacDiarmid memorial. After a mile or so winding along an exposed, boggy hillside track I arrived at a huge metal sculpture of an open book. Birds and trees and a crescent moon were cut out of the bronze and steel. It looked like a visual representation of *Under Milk Wood* in rusty auburn. It was hard to tell if the sculptor, Jake Harvey, had intended the colour, or if it was the effect of three decades spent sitting on a bed of heather exposed to the Dumfriesshire elements. Some Scottish nationalists feted the MacDiarmid memorial. During the referendum, one pro-independence website ran a three-minute video of it backed by lachrymose Celtic strings. But the metal frame erected on this barren hillside mainly spoke to me about the ambivalence of Langholm towards its *enfant terrible*. The town that largely shunned MacDiarmid in life had given him a monument in death – but as far away from its stolid, clean-living people as it possibly could. The wind was picking up. I took a quick photograph and left.

A few hours and some 40 miles later, I pulled into a car park for the William Wallace monument near Dryburgh Abbey outside St Boswells. Rain had started to pour and the thick carpet of leaves on the tarmac was heavy and sodden. In the corner of the enclosure was a small plaque. The memorial, it said, had been erected in 1814 at the behest of David Steuart Erskine, the 11th Earl of Buchan, an eccentric promoter of all things Scottish. The nearby statue, the plaque continued, 'seems to be the earliest monument to Wallace, that near legendary symbol of Scottish nationalism'. The 'near' had been crossed out in angry blue biro.

William Wallace had fought the English in the Wars of Independence and was appointed Guardian of Scotland in 1297. His story was half forgotten until the late 18th century, when it enjoyed a revival not as part of some proto-Scottish independence movement but on the back of the poetry of Burns and the prose of arch-unionist and Borders devotee, Sir Walter Scott, who is buried at the nearby ruined Dryburgh Abbey. Wallace memorials began to proliferate across Scotland. In 1861, 80,000 people gathered at Stirling for a Wallace celebration. Such passionate stirrings, as Iain Macwhirter has written, 'were not seen in any way as a threat to the Union.' Victorians in Scotland and England celebrated Wallace as a fighter for liberty, not Scottish statehood.

This interest in Scottish medieval history dissipated in the 20th century, particularly after the Second World War. But it re-emerged again in the 1960s, especially among the ever-increasing numbers of Scottish nationalists who stood solemnly among the Tartan standards at the annual Bannockburn commemorations. From the 18th century onwards the Wallace myth had become an important part of the story of Scotland (and of Scotland's distinctiveness as a country. That Scotland is a country – that vaguest of geo-political descriptors – was one of the few facets of the 'Scottish Question' on which both sides in the referendum campaign agreed.) Stories like that of William Wallace are integral to building a sense of shared cultural and political values. Without this 'self-awareness', the scholar of nationalism Walker Connor has argued, few nations can survive, and even fewer can ever come into being in the first place. Or, in the case of Scotland, re-emerge second time around.

William Wallace, Dryburgh

That rainy afternoon a few weeks before the referendum, as I trudged towards the Dryburgh statute of Wallace, I fell into step with a trio of Indian tourists. They were a married couple and a family cousin, all around my age, who had travelled up from London where they were all working. It was their first time in Scotland.

'I love Scotland. I want to come and live here,' said the husband. He had seen the film *Braveheart* and read about the Dryburgh statue in the guidebook that was folded under his arm.

At the end of the short, tree-lined path we came into a clearing. Above us towered a 21 and a half foot figure of Wallace. Rendered in red sandstone the statue is lifeless in a stilted, Greco-Roman sort of way. The proportions are all wrong. An over-sized, block-shaped Wallace leans with his right hand on a sword, a shield hanging from his left. He wears a look of bored confusion, as if unsure what he is doing perched on a pedestal overlooking the Tweed but doesn't much care either way. The Indian visitors, however, seemed pleased. They smiled and took lots of photographs: 'It's great, really great.'

* * *

As a historical reference point for Scots that is largely without meaning for the English, Flodden serves as a reminder that the different countries and regions of these isles are products of diverse and even conflicting histories which define and distinguish us as much as they point to a shared past.

MICHAEL BROWN, *London Review of Books*, 23 January 2014

On 9 September 1513, James IV led a Scottish army into battle against a smaller English force near Branxton in Northumberland. In the preceding weeks, James had seized the opportunity afforded by Henry VIII's military expedition in France to attack the 'auld enemy'. He had taken numerous English border posts with ease. By the time the Scottish army arrived at Flodden they had more men and more weapons than their English opponents. They also held the most propitious ground. But the battle was a disaster. The English forces led by Thomas Howard, Earl of Surrey, decisively outflanked the Scots. James was hacked to death. Alexander, his 20-year-old illegitimate son died too, along with many of Scotland's noblemen and clergy and over 10,000 foot soldiers. Flodden was, for some of the participants, an extension of the old Border skirmishing. A large contingent of Surrey's archers – who caused such devastation to the Scots – came from South Tynedale.

Defeat for Scotland, historian Michael Brown wrote, left a formerly 'confident, cultured and stable kingdom' to become 'a pawn of the larger realms of England, France and Spain.' The name 'Flodden' resonated balefully through the ages of Scottish history, a battle constantly refought in melancholic verse and folk memories. Flodden did not spell the end of Scotland's independence, but it was the beginning of the end.

It is not hard to imagine what the topography of Flodden would have looked like to the competing armies of James and Surrey. Where Bannockburn is nestled amongst streets filled with unremarkable new build semis and Glencoe teems with hikers and day-trippers, Flodden appears almost untouched by the intervening centuries. On a blustery Saturday morning I walked up to the battlefield. The grass was short and the roads that led to the Flodden car park were empty. In every direction rows of tidy, well-kept green fields peeled out, punctuated by the occasional farmhouse. To the south, the Cheviots proudly rose. The only sound, save the wind, was a thresher in the distance. Beyond that shiny white turbines rotated on Scottish soil. I tried to place on the horizon the invisible border that separates Scotland and England, which snakes and juts unpredictably in this corner of Northumberland. I couldn't. I walked to the brow of the hill, in the centre of the field, where there stands a large, bare granite Celtic cross. Half a millennium earlier the Scots had given up these quiet slopes and, under fire from English cannon, advanced into the boggy valley, where the English routed them. 'To the brave of both nations' read an inscription below the monument. A single wreath had fallen off and lay flaking on the concrete. The cross was erected in 1910, funded by public subscription ahead of the 400th anniversary of the battle.

Flodden memorial, looking north towards Scotland

In 2013, there was little appetite for permanent Flodden memorials. But around £1m was spent on various activities and initiatives to commemorate the 500th anniversary. Dozens of 16th century documents pertaining to the battle were transcribed and archaeological excavations were conducted in the hope of establishing exactly where the fighting had taken place. A special Flodden beer was brewed. On my way back from the battle site, I stopped at Branxton, the quaint hamlet that can be seen from the Flodden memorial. It looked like my mental image of Ambridge, the fictional village where *The Archers* is set. A St George's Cross flew in the garden of a large, detached house. Nearby, the door was ajar at St Paul's, a small church that has stood in the village since the 12th century. I opened the wooden gate. Just inside a sign said that 'after the battle of Flodden in 1513 our ancient parish church of Branxton received the slain of both nations'. The script was in medieval, serif-heavy font, a digital age mock-up of the calligraphic flourishes found in venerable manuscripts. Across the grass footpath a note pinned inside a glass-cased noticeboard advertised the 'Vicars and Tarts Vintage Tractor Rally' the following weekend.

The church was empty inside. Two rows of half a dozen hard wood pews reflected the morning light. On the wall facing the pulpit hung a framed montage of photographs of what appeared to be different parishioners holding floral displays. In one shot, a middle-aged woman smiled as she cradled an armful of roses. In another an elderly man and what could have been his wife stood beside a tidy bouquet arranged in the shape of a Saltire. Below the pictures, a narrow band of text explained that these were images from a 'flower festival' for 'peace, reconciliation and healing'. It reminded me of the kind of thing I used to see often in Belfast when I worked on community relations projects between republicans and loyalists. But here the enmity hardly seemed real. How much healing is needed between the people of Northumberland and their neighbours across the Tweed?

The previous evening I had spent the night in a onetime railway worker's cottage near Midfield, adjacent to a long discontinued Borders rail line in Northumberland. The owner, John Hardy, was a thin, energetic northerner who had lived for 15 years in Haddington, near Edinburgh. His grandfather, Edward, had been a Labour MP in Manchester, and was the first candidate returned in the landslide 1945 general election. His grandson was wary of the upcoming referendum on the border: 'A lot of the shopkeepers around here are worried. And people are worried about house prices, too.'

In her aptly titled book *States of Union and Disunion*, Linda Colley described the UK as a 'state nation' that operates on two distinct levels: its leaders protect the autonomy and separateness of the various parts, but at same time foster and sustain a shared sense of belonging. The rise of Scottish nationalism strongly suggested that this approach was breaking down, at least in places. Colley wrote:

> Arguably it has been a growing failure since the Second World War to keep renovated this kind of two-level strategy [...] that lies behind some of the United Kingdom's current dissensions.

That, of course, is not to say that the idea of the Union as mutually constituted and mutually beneficial is dead – much as its detractors might rush to declare it moribund. The Union – and the idea of Great Britain – still has a pull. And nowhere more so than around the Border.

From Flodden, I crossed back into Scotland at Coldstream, 15 miles inland from the formerly Scottish town of Berwick-Upon-Tweed. 'Welcome to Coldstream – The First True Border Toon' declared a road sign just over the stone bridge that spans the River Tweed. On the High Street, a row of Saltires flew from the railings of a small cark park. Further down the street, a Union Flag with 'Better Together' printed across it occupied most of a shop window display. Below it the faces of Alex Salmond and Nicola Sturgeon had been superimposed onto a pair of cartoon sheep, with a placard that said 'don't let this pair pull the wool over your eyes.' The shop's owner was an amiable septuagenarian named, almost inevitably, Jock.

'I'm against, definitely against,' he said, shaking his head when I asked about the upcoming vote. He went on to tell a long story about Welsh rugby fans travelling every year to Coldstream to watch the Six Nations in the local pubs. They all rooted for whoever was playing England, he said, but that was no reason to leave the Union.

Coldstream was destroyed at least twice during the Border Wars. But today there are few signs of disquiet with the near neighbours. Indeed Coldstream felt like the most unionist place in Scotland that I visited during the campaign. There were Yes posters in some of the narrow terraced houses that lined the crowded High Street, but for once they were equalled, if not outnumbered, by 'No Thanks' signs. Coldstream has a strong, material connection with the Union. It is the only town in the UK with its own army regiment. I visited the local museum, which was almost completely dedicated to the Coldstream Guards. There were mannequins of men in military dress and mementos from both world wars. Back on the High Street, I called into an army surplus store called Walk This Way. The rails were filled with khakis and military fatigues, gas masks and army boots. The basement housed a collection of the kind of equipment that would have been used in Winston Churchill's 'secret bunker' during the Second World War. (The 'secret bunker' was located in Fife.) The shop's owner, Trevor Brunning, was an army veteran as well.

Coldstream

'I think it's a sad thing that we've come to this point. I'd like to see Scotland staying in the union,' Brunning, a father of four from North London, said. 'From my standpoint, I don't see what the benefit would be of leaving.'

Just off the High Street, I walked through Henderson Park, an attractive slice of land adorned with perfectly straight flowerbeds and excellent views over the River Tweed and, beyond it, the Cheviot Hills of Northumberland. On the English side of the river, buzzards circled. The park had been built to commemorate a visit by the Queen and the Duke of Edinburgh in 1962. It was opened by Alec Douglas Home, and the former Prime Minister is buried nearby. The Perth constituency he held with such a resounding majority now returns a Scottish Nationalist MP to Westminster, Pete Wishart, a onetime keyboard player with Celtic rock band Runrig.

On 18 September, there were no surprises in southern Scotland. Dumfries and Galloway voted no by 65.7 per cent to 34.3. The result in the Scottish Borders was even more emphatic. Only Shetland, more than 100 miles from the nearest clod of the Scottish mainland, rejected independence by a greater margin. About a month after the vote, I passed through Coldstream again. It was the only place in Scotland that I saw where people still had 'No Thanks' stickers in their windows.

CHAPTER FOUR

Catalonia Dreaming

Catalonia and Scotland have enough personality to follow their own ways.

ARTUR MAS, President of the Generalitat of Catalonia,
January 2014

ALL NATIONALISMS have their myths. Often these take the form of inspiring anecdotes harking back to historical struggles. In countries that achieve statehood, the heroic battle is generally won. The signatories of the Declaration of Independence went on to win their freedom from Britain. Britain itself defeated the Nazis in the Second World War. Sometimes the confrontations that ring through the ages are lost. (The Serbs, for example, were vanquished by Ottoman forces at Kosovo Polje.) Such storied defeats are particularly formative in what Scottish sociologist David McCrone would call 'stateless nations'. Long before independence was won, Ireland celebrated the United Irishmen that were routed in 1798. Bonnie Prince Charlie has a special pull on Scottish heartstrings. In Catalonia, and Catalan nationalism, there is one reversal that, above all others, has never been forgotten: the siege of Barcelona.

The siege of Barcelona, which lasted for a year and two months, finally ended on 11 September 1714, when the city fell to Bourbon forces. The defeat effectively ended the War of Spanish Succession and, with it, Catalan self-rule. The victorious Felipe V enacted the *Neuva Planta* decrees, annulling Catalan laws and institutions. Barcelona's university was closed and all writing and teaching in the Catalan language was forbidden. The entire region was cast into a fug of bitterness and frustration that, three centuries later, it is still struggling to negotiate its way through.

11 September became *La Diada*, Catalonia's national holiday.

Franco banned *La Diada*. The Spanish dictator also outlawed the Catalan national anthem, 'Els Segadors'. The history of the nation-state is also a history of what happens when sub-state nationalist sentiment in suppressed. It festers and it grows. On 11 September 1977, just two years after the *Caudillo* died, one million people gathered in Barcelona calling for autonomy. Public space was Catalan again.

Fast-forward 35 years, to 11 September 2012. One and a half million people are out on the streets of Barcelona. But this time they don't want autonomy; they want independence. News wires beam images of a city bedecked in Catalan red and yellow across the globe.

For the following year, Catalan nationalists decided on a different tack. Having done the mass demonstration, for the 2013 *Diada* they would create a human chain, the '*Via Catalana*', stretching 250 miles across the region from the French border to neighbouring Valencia. There was a conscious precedent, the 'Baltic Way', which ran through Latvia, Lithuania and Estonia in August 1989. Just months later the Berlin Wall fell and history, in the Francis Fukuyama version, ended with a victory for liberal democracy. Determination of the self, it seemed, had replaced the self-determination of nations. And yet two and half decades later sub-state nationalist movements are not only still around, they are growing.

As two of the largest independence movements in Europe, Catalan and Scottish nationalists have long made common cause. The SNP has often been wary of antagonising Madrid by issuing public declarations of support for Catalan independence, but there are strong links between activists from both movements. In September 2014, just a few days before Scots went to the polls, Catalan President Arthur Mas told British reporters, 'I would like a Yes vote in Scotland'. Unlike Westminster, the Spanish government has steadfastly refused to allow Catalonia to hold a referendum on its constitutional future. The more Madrid says No, the greater the demand for independence grows.

* * *

In Barcelona, 11 September 2013 was a warm afternoon. I stood in the spiky shadow of Gaudi's unfinished Sagrada Familia, just north of the city centre. Gaudi, who refused to speak Spanish, designed the cathedral 'to induce the powers of heaven to have pity on Catalonia'. Now it was being induced to force the world – and the Spanish state – to look at Catalonia. At exactly 5.14pm what sounded like a starter's pistol fired. Thousands linked arms amid chants of '*In, inde, independencia*'. A middle-aged man's T-shirt carried a blunt message: 'Catalonia is not Spain'. Posters in Catalan called for 'Independence to Change Everything'. Drones flew overhead, employed not by the Spanish government but by *independenistas* to film the human chain as it snaked its way across Catalonia. The event was a remarkable feat of logistics, organisation and political mobilisation, although I thought the symbolism – particularly the equation of Madrid with Communist Moscow – a little churlish. Nobody seemed to share my disquiet.

La Diada, Barcelona, 11 September 2013

'I feel different. I think in Catalan. I don't think in Spanish,' Francesc, a 20-something law student told me as he stood in the line encircling La Sagrada. 'I feel happy today. I feel like I am with people who feel like me, who talk like me,' he continued. 'If I live to see my country free, I will be happy'.

His girlfriend nodded. Nearby a sausage dog tugged on his leash. The *gos* was wrapped in the *Esteldada*, the starry Catalan independence flag inspired by Cuba's revolutionary standard.

Identities are not innate and predetermined but constructed and, crucially, performed. We are what we do, as feminist philosopher Judith Butler recognised. Performing identity is an integral part of showing others who we are. A little further along the human chain outside La Sagrada, a young punk sported a Mohawk, a nose ring and a Catalan flag.

In 2006, John Hooper, *The Guardian*'s former Spain correspondent, wrote in his book, *The New Spaniards*:

> Catalan dissatisfaction has, for the most part, tended to be expressed as resentment, indignation and a demand for a substantial say in the running of their own affairs, rather than in terms of outright separatism.

This temperate attitude has changed. In June 2005, just 13.6 per cent of Catalans wanted independence. Opinion polls conducted in October 2014 found almost half in favour of forming a new state outside Spain. A research centre funded by the nationalist-dominated Catalan government compiled the data, but you don't need to be a psephologist – or even a particularly keen watcher of Spanish politics – to recognise a definite shift in popular opinion. In 2007, support for Catalan independence was barely a fifth. Possibly more importantly, Catalan's sense of identity is in flux, too. In 2009, less than 20 per cent said they felt 'Catalan only'. Last year that figure was 31 per cent. The number feeling 'more Spanish than Catalan' has fallen in consort. Support for maintaining the constitutional status quo has plummeted to just 23 per cent.

The clamour for independence can be attributed to a number of factors: Spain's financial travails; growing anger at cash transfers from prosperous Catalonia to poorer regions; a strengthening sense of a distinctive Catalan identity and politics; and widespread frustration with the central government's reluctance to grant more powers to the Catalan Parliament, which was re-established in 1980.

'If Madrid wanted to defuse or confuse this independence movement they would immediately offer a federal package to Catalonia,' English-born writer Matthew Tree, who I had been chatting with on Twitter in the weeks leading up to *La Diada*, told me when we bumped into each other outside La Sagrada as the human chain broke up.

'But they can't do it because they have been whipping up anti-Catalan sentiment and making political capital from it.'

Madrid has, so far, shown no sign that it is minded to negotiate with separatists. During the referendum campaign, Spanish premier Mariano Rajoy was often the international *bête noire* of Scottish nationalists. A rather dour Conservative, Rajoy frequently intimated that Spain would block a prospective independent Scotland's attempts to join the European Union. Rajoy feared that Scottish secession would give succour to Catalan nationalists.

In May 2013, Artur Mas wrote to Rajoy, asking for permission to hold a referendum in Catalonia. He had to wait four months for a reply. Rajoy rejected the request out of hand. 'The ties that bind us together cannot be undone without enormous cost,' he wrote. 'We need to work together to strengthen these ties and move away from confrontation.'

But Catalonia, according to Matthew Tree, has already slipped its binds with the Spanish state, if they ever firmly held her in the first place. 'I've never had a sense that I'm living in Spain. It's not just the language, it's a whole different place. It is a separate country,' he commented.

A group of five young men walked past us. Each was wearing the latest Barcelona FC away strip, based on the gold and red of the *Senyera*, the Catalan flag. Tree, a stocky man with a Northerner's easy manner, has lived in Catalonia for almost three decades. He came with his first wife, a Catalan. The marriage ended after two years, but he stayed on.

'The more I started reading in Catalan, the more I discovered that it is a whole cultural universe. And no-one knows about it.' If Catalan calls for greater autonomy are ignored now, the demand for full independence could grow into a deafening roar, Tree told me. Drums began to beat in the distance. 'If this isn't sorted out now, it will just go on and on and on. The cat is out of the bag now'.

A few days later, Scottish nationalists met in Edinburgh for a pro-independence rally. An estimated 15,000 people gathered on the Royal Mile and marched up Calton Hill. The train was colourful and largely good-natured, but in the 'Athens of the North' there seemed little of the passionate intensity that had characterised *La Diada*. It would only be in the very last weeks of the referendum campaign – in places such as Glasgow's George Square – that Scottish nationalism would produce anything close to a mass protest movement.

* * *

Barcelona is unusual. It is, as Colm Toibin noted, 'the only city in the world which was powerful during the 14th century and not afterwards'. Indeed, the city's heyday arguably came even earlier. In 1137, Barcelona, which had already subsumed much of Catalonia, was joined by marriage to the Kingdom of Aragon. The new union went on to conquer Valencia and the Balearic Islands during the 13th century. The Catalan-Aragonese federation controlled Sardinia, Corsica and large swathes of Greece. Their royal family even sat on the throne of Sicily, where to this day naughty children are warned to 'do what I say or I'll call the Catalans'. It was not for nothing, that Jordi Pujol, President of the autonomous Catalan government declared in Barcelona in the spring of 1988, 'From here we ruled Athens'.

Barcelona remains a powerful city, with pockets of significant wealth. Its middle and upper classes emerged relatively unscathed from both the Spanish Civil War and Franco's stifling dictatorship. Catalonia was among the first parts of Spain to be industrialised. Today, it is the country's most prosperous and most economically productive region and accounts for more than a quarter of Spain's tax take – far more than its share of Spain's population. In 2012, Catalonia's fiscal deficit – the difference between what it pays to Madrid and, after taking some funds to pay state costs, the money it gets back – was £13bn (around 8 per cent of the region's GDP), according to the Catalan government. Such disparities have deepened resentment. One pro-independence textbook that I was given not long after arriving in Barcelona in 2013 talked of 'fiscal pillaging' by Madrid.

The Catalan capital, in places, retains an air of old money that is absent from, say, Glasgow or Manchester. There are yachts moored at Barceloneta. The city's most expensive street, Passeig de Gràcia, is an impressive avenue lined with chic fashion houses and jewellery stores. Halfway down stands Casa Batlló, Gaudi's undulating blue and azure tiled masterpiece, built as the family home for a textile magnate at the turn of the century. The streets running off Passeig de Gràcia are filled with boutiques and upmarket cafes. It was in one of these that I met Carles Boix, professor of politics and public affairs at Princeton University and a close confidante of Catalonia's nationalist government. Boix speaks with the self-assured air of a man who is used to being listened to. He seemed to have little doubt that Catalonia's constitutional future lies outside Spain.

'Catalonia has tried to live within Spain in a politically organised way for 100 years. There have been many movements to gain autonomy but this autonomy has always been very restrictive. We have tried to reform the Spanish state but that has not worked,' he said.

Catalonia has a long – and rather tortured – history of self-government. The region never had a king, but was instead ruled by the Counts of Barcelona for nine centuries up until that fateful day, 11 September 1714. The Count, in 1068, codified the law into *ustages* setting out the rights and duties of the sovereign. There are parallels with the Declaration of Arbroath. The *ustages*, Colm Toibin wrote:

> later became part of the nationalist dream which saw this early definition of rights as the beginning of the tradition of individual freedom of which the Catalans claim part.

By the beginning of the 13th century, Catalonia had a *Corts* or parliament with three chambers – one each for the nobility, the bourgeoisie and the clergy.

In 1640, the Catalans and the Portuguese rebelled against Madrid. Even after the fall of Barcelona in 1714, Catalan aspirations proved difficult to tame. As Spain began to centralise in the 19th century, organising itself into departments along French lines, movements for Catalan autonomy grew in popularity. In the early 20th century – as Asquith was proposing 'Home Rule all round' as the solution to Britain's 'Irish Question' – a provincial administration was created in Catalonia. This lasted barely a decade before being abolished by aristocratic dictator Primo De Rivera. In 1931, the year after De Rivera went into exile and died, a new party of radical nationalists won municipal elections in Catalonia. Their leader, a septuagenarian named Francesc Macià, immediately declared Catalonia a republic as part of an Iberian federation – a political formation that did not even exist. Central government in Madrid persuaded Macià to tone down the secessionist rhetoric. He was rewarded with an autonomous parliament, the Generalitat, named after the medieval institution of the same name. The new government made Catalan an official language. Public spending on social provision increased.

This brief 'golden age' of Catalan Home Rule beat a staccato rhythm. In 1934, the Cortes in Madrid suspended the Generalitat and appointed a governor general to take over its functions. Members of the Catalan Parliament were each sentenced to 30 years in prison. In February 1936, the newly elected left-wing Popular Front government issued an amnesty, and the Catalan statute of autonomy was restored. Catalonia quickly became the cockpit of the republican effort in the nascent civil war, and, as the anti-Franco forces were pushed back, Barcelona became the capital of the ever-diminishing Republic. When the city finally fell, Lluís Companys, President of the Generalitat, fled to France. He was arrested by the Gestapo and repatriated to an expectant Franco, who promptly had him shot in 1940 at Montjuic, in Barcelona. Companys' last words were '*Visca Catalunya*!', 'Long Live Catalonia!'.

The death of Franco in 1975 brought democracy to Spain and put autonomy – the Catalan desire that dare not speak its name – back onto the political agenda. When aged Catalan leader, Josep Tarradellas, formerly a minister in the wartime Republican administration in Barcelona, returned from exile in 1977, he proclaimed '*Ja so aqui*' ('I have made it'). But through the '80s and the '90s, Catalans grew unhappy with the limits of the self-government that they were given in the shiny, early days of the new Republic. Unlike their Basque cousins, Catalonia had almost no fiscal autonomy. The 1992 Olympics transformed Barcelona, but the Generalitat largely stayed the same.

In 2004, Socialist leader José Luis Rodríguez Zapatero surprised the Spanish political establishment by winning the general election. Zapatero initially supported a new statute for Catalan autonomy, which had been drawn up by the left wing regional government at the time. This settlement made Catalan the senior official language above Castilian Spanish and averred that 'the parliament of Catalonia has defined Catalonia as a nation'. The statute was supported by over 73 per cent of the Catalan electorate in a referendum in June 2006. 'Discussion of the region's medium-term future ended,' wrote another erstwhile *Guardian* Spain correspondent, Giles Tremlett, at the time. Catalonia's constitutional destiny had been secured – except it hadn't. Zapatero's enthusiasm for the new deal for Catalonia quickly cooled. The Prime Minister said that he could not endorse anything that would undermine the unity of Spain. The conservative opposition People's Party launched a legal challenge.

The debate at the Constitutional Court dragged on for four years. Eventually the law lords struck out 14 of the statute's 277 articles as 'unconstitutional' and watered down many others.

Catalans have a reputation as a phlegmatic, level-headed people, but their reaction to the Constitutional Court's decision was swift. The full ruling was released on 9 July 2010. The following day a huge demonstration took place in Barcelona. Estimates of the numbers involved varied widely – organisers said 1.5 million, police put the figure at 1.1 million, Madrid-based newspaper *El País* reported 425,000 – but regardless, a new mythical moment in the history of Catalan nationalism had occurred. The nationalist genie was out of the bottle, and has, so far, refused to go back in.

One place where this new political dispensation is particularly apparent is Girona, an orderly, well-to-do Roman city an hour or so northeast of Barcelona. When I visited a few days after the 2013 *Diada*, the Pont de Pedra, a sturdy stone bridge over a slow flowing river, was lined with Catalan flags.

'There is real resentment at how Catalonia hasn't changed,' Edward Hugh, a Liverpudlian who came to Spain to teach English and never left, told me over a bowl of *gazpacho*, the cold tomato soup that the Moors brought to Spain from the Maghreb.

Since the financial crisis, Hugh has put his first training, as a London School of Economics-educated economist, to use. As we walked through the Call, Girona's old Jewish quarter, he quoted facts and figures about Catalan exports and VAT take, competitive advantage and regional economies. 'Catalonia is a rich county,' he said. 'Independence now is an irresistible force.'

In Catalonia, almost all social and economic issues are increasingly refracted through the prism of the national question. Take the Jewish history that Girona proudly boasts. The Call is one of the best-preserved Jewish quarters in Europe (in part because most of the Jews were expelled in the 15th century). There are a host of plaques and a museum of Catalan Jewish life. But there is a discernably political motive in this celebration of difference, too. By emphasising the Jewish presence – what Colm Toibin called 'its non-Arab influences' – Catalonia is also stressing its separateness from the rest of Spain, which came under the sway of the Moors for centuries.

Catalan distinctiveness is most obviously expressed through language. Around 6.5 million people now speak Catalan. Debates about the relationship between language and nationalism have been well rehearsed, but Catalan, and the culture that grew up around it, is certainly an integral part of the independence sales pitch. This would have seemed incredibly unlikely four decades ago. By the time Franco died, Catalan was in crisis. Massive post-war immigration had brought an influx of non-speakers to Catalonia, often to work in the industrial heartlands. More than that, since Catalan had not been taught in schools, many speakers were illiterate in the language. At the same time, as native Catalans married immigrants, the language was used less often in the home than it was in public, a reversal of most minority languages.

After the resumption of the Generalitat, Catalan was given priority in the region's education system. Now, it is in the ascendancy. (Although the younger generation is increasingly trilingual, adding English to their Castilian.) Joan Miró and Antoni Tàpies bequeathed Catalans a visual lexicon of independence, too, while in recent years overtly 'Catalanist' media outlets have proliferated. The television station TV3 was created in the 1980s to promote the Catalan language. The newspaper ARA was founded in 2010 with a pro-independence editorial line. By 2013, the paper had daily print sales of 27,520 and more than 1.7million online readers.

Madrid, recognising too late the link between cultural nationalism and its political variant, adopted a heavy-handed approach. In 2012, Jose Ignacio Wert, Spain's Education Minister, unveiled proposals that all coursework in Catalan schools must be offered in Spanish and Catalan 'in balanced proportions'. For many Catalans, even those with little interest in constitutional change, these pronouncements evoke divisive memories of the Spanish Civil War and their language's suppression under Franco.

At the same time, Catalan nationalists, like their Scottish cousins, have placed less emphasis on culture and more on the practical need for greater self-government. In 2008, Josep-Luis Carod-Rivera, then leader of the Republican Left of Catalonia (ERC), wrote that, 'being and feeling Spanish in Catalonia, more or much more Spanish than Catalan in Catalonia – even perhaps *just* Spanish – is perfectly compatible with arguing for Catalan independence.'

Catalonia's 14th century glory days were ended by a banking collapse in 1381. Now a financial crisis has provided the backdrop for the re-emergence of Catalan nationalism. Spain, on the back of a massive housing boom, suffered one of the worst crashes in Europe. In 2012, the government in Madrid was forced to take out around €100bn (£80bn) in bailout loans, and introduce unpopular austerity measures. Unemployment skyrocketed, especially amongst the young. The loosely nationalist political parties that dominated the Catalan Parliament for more than 30 years – Artur Mas' centrist Convergèn-cia i Unió (Convergence and Union) and the more openly pro-seces-sionist ERC – were also forced to respond. Although the word 'inde-pendence' rarely featured in government pronouncements, a new vision of Catalan statehood started to emerge. On the back of the huge *Diada* rally in Barcelona, Arthur Mas called snap elections in November 2012. Separatists won a clear majority. Mas was returned once more as premier but his party lost a fifth of their seats. The Republican Left, however, doubled their representation.

Catalonia's politicians are 'riding a tiger they cannot control', veteran Catalan nationalist Alfons Lopez Tena said over lunch in a Barcelona restaurant called Pitarra – the pen name used by 19th century satirist and Catalanist Federico Soler. A short man with a bright blue jacket that looked like something a croupier would wear, Lopez Tena was clearly agitated by what he perceived as the timidity of the city's political classes. 'They say "we want a state of our own", but what does that mean? Some days a state of their own is Denmark. On other days it is a state of their own like Massachusetts.'

In September 2014, the Government of Catalonia announced that they would hold a referendum on independence. Voters would be asked a question with two parts: 'Do you want Catalonia to become a State?' and 'In case of an affirmative response, do you want this State to be independent?' The plebiscite was to take place on Sunday 9 November.

Within days, the Spanish constitutional court, reacting to a request from Madrid, suspended the proposed referendum. Mas announced that his government would instead hold a formal but non-binding 'consultation' – which in turn was blocked by the courts. Instead more than 40,000 volunteers organised a 'participatory process', printing ballot slips and election literature and setting up voting booths in schools across Catalonia. Thousands of Catalans came from all around the world to participate in what was essentially a mass opinion poll. In all more than 2.35 million Catalans cast a ballot. Over 80 per cent answered *si-si* (yes-yes) to the double-barrelled question. Almost of all of those who want to remain part of Spain stayed at home. Madrid declared the vote illegal and threatened to prosecute its organisers, and Artur Mas.

* * *

The night before the September 2013 *Diada*, I took the subway to Sants, a working class nationalist stronghold west of the city centre. I emerged from the underground on to an almost deserted street. I had been told that there would be a torch lit procession for independence, but all I could see were slow moving cars and elderly dog walkers. Further up the street, a faint sound of chanting came from an open door. I followed the noise, through another door and, eventually, into a large, glass-fronted auditorium. On a raised central stage a bearded man with a paunch and a younger, attractive woman were leading a chorus of the *Internationale*. An elderly woman in front of me had her eyes shut tight, her lips moving in time with the song. Around the hall, clenched fists were raised in unison. The whole scene had the feel of a religious revival. Catalan, Basque and Communist flags were pinned to the walls.

After the song finished the room emptied out into a nearby square. I followed. Blazing bull rushes illuminated the night. A drum beat out an incessant rhythm. There were starry *Esteldada* standards and t-shirts imploring, 'Keep Calm and Speak Catalan.' As the procession got underway, along a narrow street, I fell into conversation with a family of independence supporters.

'Will you be in the human chain tomorrow?' I asked.

'Yes', father, mother and two teenager girls shouted almost in unison. The eldest child had a Catalan flag pendant around her neck and earrings in the shape of the three-pronged peace symbol. She would turn 18 later that week.

'We don't feel respected about our language and our way of life,' her mother, Jemina Albesa, told me as we began to shuffle forward. We quickly fell into talking, not about Catalonia but about her life. She was born in Uruguay to middle class Spanish parents.

'We had a big house, a big car, servants at home. We went to the British school. We had a good life there.' But her parents also had another life. They were members of the Tupamaros, a left wing group that fought an urban guerrilla war in Uruguay in the 1960s and 1970s. In August 1972, the military came for her father and mother. They spent two years in prison. Both were tortured. After

Catalan independence poster, Barcelona

their release the family moved to Sitges, a resort town near Barcelona now popular with the gay community. Jemina arrived in Spain on 20 March 1975. 'I never forget that date'.

'Why did they join the Tupamaros?' I asked as the smell of burning rushes gave the warm evening air a sharp taste.

'It was my mother,' Jemina said, stopping and grabbing my arm. 'Her conscience.' She puffed out her chest. 'She was like, "I can carry the world on my shoulders".'

Around us there was fire and solemn chants of '*In, inde, independencia.*' It felt like *semana santa*, Spain's holy week, minus the white Ku Klux Klan hoods and the religious iconography.

The procession came to a halt in an open square ringed by public housing about a mile from Sants. It was after 9.00pm but children sat on swings in an adjacent playground. The square quickly filled up as a contingent arrived from the nearby neighbourhood of Poble Sec. Everyone started to clap and chant. I lost Jemina and her family in the throng. I pushed my way to the front, where a short woman was burning a piece of paper. It was a copy of Felipe V's notorious anti-Catalan *Neuva Planta* decrees. When the parchment had been reduced to ashes the crowd applauded. Then a group of awkward looking teenagers carrying musical instruments took to the stage and played the Catalan nationalist anthem. After that the crowd thinned out. Tomorrow was another day.

The climax of *La Diada*, the following evening, was an open-air concert at the Arc De Triomf, the triumphal arch that presides over Passeig de Lluís Companys. Crowds of young Catalans milled about as rock bands played accompanied by fire works and over-excited light shows. Immigrants in groups of twos and threes sold ready mixed cocktails. Towards the back of the large crowd, I met a man in his late 30s with a clipped English accent. He wore a 'People's Republic of Cork' t-shirt and had the slightly haggard look of someone who had spent a decade teaching English in Barcelona.

Estelada flies from Arc de Triomf,
Barcelona, 11 September 2013

'Which part of England are you from?' I asked, making conversation.

He looked wounded. 'I'm not from England, I'm from Cornwall,' he said, pausing to take a sip from his mojito. 'But I was brought up over the border. In Devon. It was terrible'.

Around us were secessionists from across Europe. There was a young man waving a Saltire, another with a Welsh dragon. Two heavy set men with square jaws and cannon-ball heads wore matching 'Piedmont' hoodies. There was a man in his 20s called Juri, who looked more like a skateboarder than 'the foreign spokesperson of the Friulian liberation movement'. He wore a white Vans cap at an angle and baggy shorts. He spoke English with a distinct Scottish twang. He lived in Hawick, in the Scottish borders, where he planted trees for a living. The previous week he had travelled to Ireland, to attend a commemoration for republican Hunger Strikers, in Donegal.

'I'll be in Dublin for a conference soon representing our movement. We are small but we are getting bigger'. I had to look Friuli up on the internet. I learned that its historical capital is Udine and Furlan, a language distinct from Italian, has around 300,000 native speakers. There was not much detail in English anywhere online about the region's liberation movement.

All these sub-state nationalist movements are – in some way – a response to crisis, whether political, economic or even existential. If small (or smaller) is not quite beautiful, it is preferable to the present order, better able to buttress the nation (however defined) against the slings and arrows of late modernity. Catalonia – like Scotland – offers hope for frustrated regional nationalists across the continent. As my Cornish interlocutor on that balmy *Diada* evening in Barcelona said, 'Scotland and Catalonia are our chance – if they don't do it we never will.'

But Scotland and Catalonia are very different places, too. Spain's asymmetric devolution might resemble the United Kingdom's piecemeal efforts to transfer power to 'the regions', but the constitutional similarities are often overplayed. Britain has a long history of parliamentary democracy. Forty years ago Spain was a dictatorship. Many Catalans talk with ambivalence about 'the Spanish state' as if it is somehow does not encompass them. Madrid's intransigence to demands for greater Catalan autonomy evinces the central state's lack of confidence, and a burgeoning crisis of legitimacy. The UK leader Catalan nationalists praise is often not Alex Salmond, but David Cameron. 'Cameron is a democrat,' they say, 'he gave Scotland a referendum'. Such an outcome still seems unthinkable in Catalonia.

Around the same time that I was watching the human chain at Sagrada Familia, a group of neo-Nazi sympathisers attacked the official ceremony in the Catalan Government Centre in Madrid. They waved pro-Franco Falangist flags and threw pepper spray, shouting '*No nos engañan, Cataluña es España*' ('They don't deceive us, Catalonia is Spain').

The night before the illegal Catalan independence poll in November 2014, I went for dinner with some Scottish nationalist commentators and activists who had come to observe proceedings. In a trendy Barcelona brewpub we drank local beer, ate Catalan tapas and talked about the unfolding situation.

'The last time I felt like where we are now in Scotland and Catalonia was in Lisbon in 1974,' said George Kerevan, a columnist in *The Scotsman* and onetime SNP councillor in Edinburgh. In 1974, the 'Carnation Revolution' brought down Portugal's longstanding dictatorship.

Kerevan and his wife, Angela, both wore matching Yes badges. He had first met with Catalan nationalists in Barcelona in 1973, when Spain was still a fascist dictatorship.

'Catalan nationalist politics was always led by the bourgeois,' he said. 'The working class is very split (on independence).'

Across the table sat Jamie Maxwell, a young Scottish nationalist-minded journalist who came to prominence during the referendum. Maxwell's father, Stephen, had been a leading member of the 79 Group, a movement in the SNP that argued Scottish nationalism needed to take a more left wing stance. Among those expelled by the SNP for joining the 79 Group was Alex Salmond. Jamie Maxwell had been following the Catalan and Scottish movements closely. He talked of 'structural differences' between the two. Whereas in Scotland, it was the largely the Scottish National Party leading the march to independence, in Catalonia civil society had made the running amid a growing public frustration with the Spanish state.

'People in Catalonia are pushing the parties to do radical things whereas in Scotland it was a constitutionally radical party pushing a rather reluctant people,' Maxwell said.

The previous night, around 10,000 people attended a final rally in Barcelona ahead of the ballot. Some of the loudest cheers of the evening were reserved for Natalie McGarry. An energetic, garrulous Glaswegian, McGarry had been one of the leading lights in the Women for Independence campaign during the referendum. She was also the SNP candidate defeated by Alex Rowley in January's Cowdenbeath by-election. In Catalonia, she was part of a small delegation from the Scottish Independence Convention observing the poll.

Some Scottish nationalists had come across on their own steam, too. A pair of friends from Ullapool spent the weekend walking around Barcelona in kilts and matching Yes t-shirts. Their photograph appeared in the Catalan edition of the Spanish daily *La Vanguardia*.

The mood on the morning of the poll was a mix of jubilation

and trepidation. Voters smiled and took photographs as they queued outside ad hoc polling stations. But many were worried that Madrid would attempt to halt the ballot. Their fears proved unfounded, although later that evening Spanish Justice Minister Rafael Catalá announced that the attorney general's office was investigating whether charges could be filed against the vast network of Catalan civil society groups involved. Catalonia, at least in the short run, was no closer to holding a legal poll on its constitutional future.

After visiting a handful of orderly polling stations across Barcelona, I retreated back to my hotel to file a couple of radio reports. I was staying on La Rambla, Barcelona's noisy main drag. Next door to the hotel was a gaudy restaurant with lurid photographs of the tourist fare it served pinned up outside. It was called Café Moka. During the Spanish Civil War, the local Stalinist police used to drink here. Towards the end of the war, as internecine left wing fighting engulfed Barcelona, George Orwell spent three days lying on a Rambla roof with his 19th-century gun trained on Café Moka. Orwell's side, the Trotskyite POUM, had their headquarters just up the street. In *Homage to Catalonia,* the acclaimed British journalist recalled:

> What the devil was happening, who was fighting whom, and who was winning, was at first very difficult to discover.

Swap the bombs for the ballot box, and Orwell could almost have been writing about Catalonia in the second decade of the 21st century.

CHAPTER 5

Fear and Loathing
in Republika Srpska

One day that will fall like a pear in our hands just as, say, Scotland
or Catalonia will also do. We are waiting for examples in Europe
of how to do this.

MILORAD DODIK, President of Republika Srpska, January 2014

THE CHEAPEST WAY to get to Bosnia was to fly to Belgrade. My flight
arrived late in the evening so I had to spend the night in the Serbian
capital. I had arranged to meet a friend of a friend, a postdoctoral
student in his early 30s named Ivan who had a head of brown hair
and an infectious laugh. Ivan brought me to a smoke-filled dive bar
near the Old Town. We sat at a rickety wooden table. Around us
posters for upcoming art exhibitions and gigs were tacked to the walls.

'So what will you do in Bosnia?' Ivan asked on our second
drink.

I would, I said, travel first to Brčko, a self-governing city near
the border with Croatia and Serbia. From there I would go to Banja
Luka, the capital of Republika Srpska, to interview Milorad Dodik.
The President of the small Bosnian Serb Republic had said that he
intended to follow Scotland's lead and hold a referendum on independence from the rest of Bosnia and Herzegovina.

Ivan was delighted. He brought his half-litre glass of Budweiser
down with a thud: 'you *must* tell me what you think of Dodik. He's
always there, he never leaves the scene.'

I had not been entirely honest with Ivan. I had contacted the
press office of the Republika Srpska government but my request for
an interview with Mr Dodik had yet to receive a response. 'Don't
worry. There should be no problem', my intermediary in Banja

Luka wrote in an email the day before I flew to Belgrade. But one week later and there was still no word from the President's office. It was my third night in Banja Luka, and I was spending it alone and bored in the only restaurant I could find that was open. It was in my hotel. The restaurant stereo played dreadful lounge-style cover versions to an empty dining room. As 'With or Without You' faded into an incongruously high-pitched rendition of Tears for Fear's 'Shout', torrential rain started to dash against the plate-glass window. It was the last week in April. It had hardly stopped raining since I had arrived in Bosnia.

* * *

Banja Luka is not an easy place to kill time in. The 1995 Dayton Peace Accords divided Bosnia and Herzegovina into two almost completely independent entities: a Croat and Bosniak-controlled Federation, with its capital at Sarajevo, and a Serb Republic administered from Banja Luka. While traces of Sarajevo's cosmopolitan history linger on, despite the violence and chaos of the 1990s, Banja Luka feels more like a regional town than a capital city. The long, wide boulevard that bisects the Bosnian Serb capital is attractive in a stolid sort of way but is far too big for a city of just 200,000 people ringed in the near distance by green hills. The shops are either gaudy or bare, or both. The clock in the concrete-encrusted main square always reads ten past nine: at this time, on 26 October 1969, a devastating earthquake struck Banja Luka. More than 60 per cent of the city was destroyed.

The rebuilt Banja Luka emerged relatively unscathed from the war in the early 1990s. Most of the socialist-era buildings survived, as they still do. The composition of the city, however, changed utterly. Before 1992 about half of the population were Serbs, now it closer to 90 per cent. On my first morning in the city I watched old men trade moves on a life-size chessboard across the road from the magnificent, gold-capped Orthodox Cathedral of Christ the Saviour. During the Second World War the occupying Croat Ustaše had completely sacked the church. A little further down the street, a man of around my age and his young son laid a wreath at a Partisan monument. Busts of 21 local men and women who died fighting the fascists ringed the statue. Their names were Serbian, Bosniak, Croatian, Slovenian and Macedonian but all the garlands were wrapped in blue, red and white ribbons. The same colours – those of the Serbian flag – dangled from almost every lamppost.

Banja Luka's squat skyline is interrupted a couple of times, most notably by a 17-storey glass and steel rectangular box that looks like a Transformer taking a break mid-metamorphosis. This is Republika Srpska Government Tower. An armed guard stood in front of a pair of huge flags. The entire third floor was given over to Prime Minister Željka Cvijanović and her entourage. But the real power in Republika Srpska (or 'RS' as most everyone calls it) has long rested on the broad shoulders of Milorad Dodik. In November 2010, Dodik swapped the Prime Minister's office for that of the President in order to maintain his iron grip on the impoverished Bosnian Serb state. Ironically, the international community aided Dodik's ascent to power in 2006; the West thought he could marginalise the Serb nationalists that were at the time rendering Bosnia

City centre, Banja Luka

ungovernable. But Dodik proved anything but malleable. Rather than improving relations between the Serb Republic and the Federation, Dodik pushed the two almost-states even further apart. Threats to hold a referendum on independence – which would almost certainly result in an overwhelming vote for the break-up of Bosnia – regularly emanate from the presidential office.

'I think it's Freudian,' said Aleksandar Trifunović as he reversed his four-wheel drive into a car park in the shadow of the grandiloquent government tower. I peered up at the phallus protruding into the night sky. The glans was cloaked in fog. I felt slightly dizzy. It was Saturday night and I had only arrived in Banja Luka a couple of hours earlier after a long bus journey through northern Bosnia. Trifunović is editor-in-chief of *Buka*, an online news portal dedicated to exposing corruption and malfeasance. He led me into a busy restaurant filled with men in sharp suits and beautiful women in designer dresses.

'Come on, let's eat.'

Trifunović, who everyone seemed to call Saša, often plays the role of unofficial opposition in Republika Srpska. He organised the first political demonstration in Banja Luka. That was in 1997. The target then was the Serb Democratic Party (SDS), the party founded by Radovan Karadžić, the Bosnian Serb zealot who, at the time of writing, is on trial for war crimes at The Hague. Now Trifunović and his small team at *Buka* try their best to hold Dodik's government to account. In early 2014, the President publicly condemned Trifunović as a 'traitor'. In a 225-page booklet entitled *The Destruction of Republika Srpska*, he was accused of working for foreign powers committed to destroying the Serb Republic.

'If you are a journalist here and you don't get a hard time then you are not doing your job right,' Saša said as he dug a spoon into a chocolate soufflé.

Earlier he had told me that he was worried about his health. He looked heavy. His face was red, his hair lank. He had been thinking about moving to Sarajevo with his young family. The pay was better in the Federation capital, Trifunović said, and there was less government interference.

'Here if you are on Dodik's side you don't have any problems. Otherwise...'

And what of the calls for Bosnian Serb independence? A stunt.

'They say a referendum would solve our problems. Our problems would start the day after a referendum.'

Afterwards I went for a postprandial drink in a crowded bar off the main square. As I waited my turn at the bar, I fell into conversation with a young woman perched on a high stool.

'This is my first time in Republika Srpska,' I half-shouted, flailing about for small talk over the noise of the house band.

Her eyes lit up, as if I had said something sharp and compelling. 'You said Republika Srpska! Most people don't even know that we exist. But we do.'

* * *

In April 2014, US magazine *Newsweek* ran a profile on Dodik. Russia had just annexed Crimea. Might Republika Srpska be about to secede, too? There was more than a smear of Vaseline on the reporter's lens. ('[W]e sat for a chat in his large, sunny office at Banja Luka, his native city.') 'The former basketball player' told the world that the Scottish independence referendum was an 'example' that he, and his people, wished to follow. But while the SNP had taken pains to frame the Scottish referendum debate in civic terms – with varying degrees of accuracy, and success – Dodik's nationalism was unashamedly ethnic.

'We don't need Bosnia,' the President told the visiting American reporter. 'It's not actually only about politics. It's mentality as well. History. The Serbs had never accepted Bosnia as a state.'

Nations, French philosopher Etienne Balibar wrote, are 'retrospective illusions' so powerful that they can blind us from the 'power of myths of national origin' that both produce and sustain them. The *Newsweek* article chose not to dwell on the material circumstances that produced Republika Srpska. Neither Dodik nor his interlocutor made mention of the tens of thousands of Bosniak Muslims felled between 1992 and 1995 to clear the path for a separate Serb Republic in Bosnia.

Through a Sarajevo-based colleague, I arranged to hire a driver in Banja Luka. He was a nervous man in his early 40s who I will call

'Goran'. We met briefly at my hotel the night that I arrived in the city. He had never worked with a journalist before and was anxious to discuss the following day's schedule. I wanted to meet some of the small number of Muslims that had fled during the war but had since returned to their former homes in what is now Republika Srpska. We agreed a route and a starting time. He smiled a wan, skittish smile. It was clear he wanted to talk more, and I had no desire to stop him. He spoke candidly, notably so for a Balkan man of his generation. He told me that he was divorced, that he had a poor relationship with his ex-wife and that he 'lives now for my daughter. She is eight and a half'. He showed me a picture of a pretty child with long blonde hair. He only earned around €250 a month.

'How can anyone live like that?' he asked plaintively.

After I left, he came running after me. 'I have Orthodox crosses in my car,' he said, almost breathless.

I was slightly startled.

'I have Orthodox crosses in my car. Should I take them down?'

I nodded. 'Yes, yes. Probably best'.

Next morning Goran drove his aging Audi – a sponge hamburger dangling from the rear view mirror – towards the town of Kozarac, an hour northwest of Banja Luka. By the side of the road, the vacant faces of abandoned houses riddled with bullet holes stared down solemnly from grassy escarpments. At every crossroad a Serbian flag fluttered in the breeze. The closer we got to Kozarac, the more nervous Goran became. At 18, he had volunteered in the Bosnian Serb army. His first posting was to Kozarac. He spoke quickly as if we might be overhead.

'Serbian paramilitaries came to kill people. I didn't like that.'

He told me that he had two deep scars on his legs.

'Muslims. But I don't blame them. It was war.'

The summer Goran volunteered, 1992, Serbs began attacking the Muslim and Croat populations of Northwestern Bosnia. The name for this brutal policy soon became known around the world: 'ethnic cleansing'. Kozarac, a neat Muslim town of around 20,000 people at the foot of a sprawling national park, was largely reduced to rubble. Thousands were taken captive, many were killed. I had read about this orgy of violence – Kozarac is the locus of journalist Ed Vulliamy's haunting account of post-war Bosnia *The War is Dead, Long Live the War* – but I never would have guessed as we drove slowly into the town centre that *this* was Kozarac. It was a quiet Sunday afternoon and there were few people on the streets. It looked like any sleepy Balkan hamlet: a shop sold buttery *burek* pastries; a dog barked; a pair of elderly men sat smoking outside a café. Goran parked outside the bakery.

'I will leave you and get some coffee. It is probably better that way.' He was worried about being a Serb in an overwhelmingly Muslim town.

Many of the houses in Kozarac have been rebuilt. But not many former residents have returned permanently. Fikret Alic is one of the few that has. His name might not be familiar, but Alic's face – or, more correctly, his torso – is. It was this tall man's emaciated, skeletal frame behind barbed war, his ribs pushing out like fingers in a glove, that became the iconic image of the Bosnian war. The photograph – taken at Trnopolje concentration camp – probably saved his life.

'That picture was taken accidently. Now I have made it my own mission to talk about it. I'm doing it for the innocent people who were killed,' Alic told me.

Alic had filled out in the intervening two decades, but he still bore the scars of the abuse he suffered. He complained about a headache and chain-smoked as he sat uneasily on the edge of his chair in the local community centre. During the Ottoman Empire, the two-storey building had housed the first school for girls in this part of Bosnia. Now its walls are lined with hundreds of pictures of Kozarac citizens killed in the war. Some are as young as one or two, others as old as 101. All share the same date: 1992.

Alic talked for over an hour. He told his entire story in meticulous detail – like someone who had been asked to recount it many times. Which he had. He explained how Serbian mercenaries had rampaged through his village in June 1992, killing his father and mother and taking him prisoner. Slowly he recounted the horror of the camps: being beaten with sticks topped with iron grinding balls; being forced to load the bodies of dead prisoners on to cattle trucks; finally, walking for days to the Bosniak army lines, when, in the face of international media pressure, he was eventually released by his Serb captors.

After the war Alic moved to Denmark, but he had to spend years defending himself against allegations that the photograph was concocted, a lie invented by the West used to damn the innocent Serb people. These conspiracy theories have been given a new life online.

'The fact is that the camps happened, the massacres happened, it's time we admitted it and moved on.' He held my gaze. I flinched a little. I find it hard to look intense pain straight in the face.

From Kozarac it was a short drive to Prijedor, a dull, poor industrial town 20 miles from the Croatian border. Along the way we passed a three-storey complex with a large banner over the main entrance: 'Model's' (sic). Over-sized photographs of women with pneumatic breasts in skimpy bikinis were pinned to the exterior walls. Goran told me that this club used to belong to Arkan, the notorious Serbian paramilitary leader with a fondness for big cats.

'He was raising Tigers here. He was a barbarian,' Goran shook his head.

In 2000, Arkan, Željko Ražnatović, was shot dead in the head in the lobby of the InterContinental Hotel in Belgrade. There were numerous rumours about who had ordered his killing: the White House, Serbian leader Slobodan Milosevic, even some of his entourage. He had made a lot of enemies in his violent life.

A few miles past Prijedor, at a village called Carakovo, we met a human rights activist called Sudbin Musić. We sat in a roadside bar called *Sidro* ('anchor'). Heavy rain was falling. The River Sana was seeping over its banks. Dark brown water swirled around the wooden stilts that supported a house beside the river. Musić, however, had another, more pressing concern. The slight, fiercely intelligent redheaded Bosniak needed to find a place to bury 50 bodies. The corpses were victims from Tomasica, a mass war grave discovered a few miles away the previous year. The grave contained the bodies of around 1,000 Bosniaks killed by Serb forces in 1992.

'Where can we put them?' Musić asked the sky as we stood in the local graveyard. In front of him were row upon row of slender white headstones decorated with Arabic lettering. Almost 400 in all.

'We don't have space for any more.' His voice sounded calm, but his eyes were ablaze with anger.

In 1992, around 3,000 people lived in Carakovo. Just 300 remain. As we drove along narrow roads lined with bracken Musić pointed at recently built houses.

'They are in Slovenia, they are in Austria. They are in the

Headstones, Carakovo

Netherlands, their neighbours are in Sweden.' We passed a ramshackle construction, its concrete peeling. 'That house is occupied. The only one on the street.'

Under the Dayton agreement all refugees have a right to return to their former homes in Bosnia. When Musić left Germany in 2000, he was one of the first to come back to Carakovo.

'Everything was destroyed, like Hiroshima. (There was) Nothing', he recalled. Over the next couple of years others returned, too. But the flow of returnees became a trickle. Then it stopped completely.

'I feel like the last Mohican here,' he said, 'I ask myself "what are you doing? Are you waiting for the next disaster?"'

The administrative centre for returnees in Prijedor is housed in the same building as the headquarters of the local branch of Karadžić's Serb Democratic Party.

'I came back home but the problem is permanent discrimination. Citizens of Bosnia-Herzegovina need to be liberated,' said Musić. 'I don't belong anywhere. We are a no man's people'.

His predictions for the future were equally grim.

'You will have in five years an ethnically clean Republika Srpska and an ethnically clean Federation under the control of the Muslims and the Croats. And all the youth will have gone abroad.'

Goran sat beside him, furiously nodding throughout.

Bosnian Serb leaders continue to deny what happened in places like Kozarac and Carakovo. Officials still obstruct attempts to locate the missing, and refuse to recognise the massacre at Srebrenica and the killings at the concentration camps. 'Milorad Dodik and Republika Srpska,' in Ed Vulliamy's words, 'play games that roll the bones of the dead like dice'. There is still no commemoration at Omarska, one of the most brutal Serb-run detention centres a few miles from Kozarac. (Bosniaks and Croats ran similar camps in their areas.) A huge iron ore mine, Omarska was bought by Britain's richest man, Lakshmi Mittal, in 2004. The mine is operational again under ArcelorMittal but the world's largest steel company has not erected any memorial on the site, citing 'lack of agreement' with local Serbs.

On our way back to Banja Luka, Goran swung hard right at the sign for Omarska. I told him we did not have to, that it was late and getting dark. I wanted to leave this place. The soaring mountains seemed to take on a menacing air in the half-light. But Goran was not to be dissuaded. The conversation at Carakovo with Sudbin Musić had stirred something in him.

'He is right. The politicians play us like fools. I have more in common with him than I do with them,' Goran said, picking up speed as he drove on.

At Omarska, we stopped at the factory gates. There was a small Serbian Orthodox Church across the road. We could go no further. Returning back through the village, the streets were now bathed in a harsh orange glare from sodium lights overhead. Goran smacked his fist against the dashboard in anger.

'Look at the light! It's like a posh suburb. In the middle of nowhere.'

Soon, we were back on the main road. It was pitch black. There were no lights on the road. I checked my emails on my phone. I had no messages. No news from Dodik.

* * *

Next morning I woke early. The rain had stopped, but there was still no word from the President's office. I called my middleman. He didn't pick up. I went for a run through the soporific city. I pelted along the wide avenue, past a bust of Tito and a gloriously modernist Catholic Church, its wave-shaped roof peaking in a huge cross. I skirted along a verdant park in late spring bloom, eventually reaching the vertiginous government tower. I stopped, staring up at it, as if expecting to catch Dodik standing by a window. I imagined I could wave up at him. Grab his attention. Force him to meet me.

Nobody appeared. I was dripping sweat on the footpath, and

the security guard with the automatic weapon was giving me the evil eye. I ran back to my hotel.

That afternoon it started to rain again. I went to visit the Museum of Republika Srpska. The museum was housed in the Chamber of Commerce and Industry near my hotel. Outside a rusting Second World War tank sat, grass creeping around its caterpillar tracks; in the lobby an inscription spoke about how '*Krajina* man' – literally 'border man', but also a synonym for Serb – had 'an instinctive artist in their souls'. Just inside the door, three yellow and blue buckets were arranged on the marble floor to catch rainwater coming in through the roof. A cigarette butt floated in one. I seemed to be the only visitor.

The museum reminded me of a trip to the Ulster Museum in Belfast about a decade earlier. Both were small, began in pre-history and took a very particular view of the more recent, contested past. Here the story of Bosnia presented was the story of the Serbs of Bosnia. A large swathe of the main hall was given over to the turn-of-the-century Balkan Wars. US journalist, John Reed, was quoted favourably, saying that this was:

> a strange country, dead and alive at the same time, devastated by war and yet showing powerful morality in battle.

> A committed socialist, Reed reported on the October Revolution in 1917. His subsequent book *Ten Days That Shook the World* became a bestseller.

The bulk of the RS Museum – around a third of the ground floor and the entire second floor – was given over to a single subject: the Independent State of Croatia, the NDH. A series of stark black and white photographs and laminated red panels recorded the atrocities committed by the Ustaše, the Croatian fascists whose wartime puppet state encompassed all of present-day Croatia and Bosnia and Herzegovina as well as significant chunks of Slovenia and Serbia. They ruled with a degree of violence and barbarity that surpassed even that of their Nazi overlords. Ustaše leader Ante Pavelić spoke of 'purifying' Croatia. At Jasenovac, about 50 miles from Banja Luka over the Croatian border, the Ustaše put this crude chauvinism into practice, building one of the largest, and most notorious, concentration camps in Europe. Between 1941 and 1945, Serbs, Jews, Roma and other 'undesirables' were slaughtered in their tens of thousands at Jasenovac. A long museum panel signed 'senior curator for contemporary history Drago Trninic' ended with:

> The tragedy of Jasenovac mustn't be forgotten. Jasenovac warns and reminds that any people in the world must not ever experience such genocide.

Mr Trninic excoriated those who contested the numbers that died at the camps for political ends. Photographs showed the crucifix, dagger, hand grenade and pistol that were held by the men who swore the Ustaše oath. There were rows of headshots of the victims of the camps. The images reminded me of the community centre in Kozarac where I had sat with Fikret Alic. The young men on both walls had similar faces, the same sharp features and serious mouths.

Ustaše victims, Museum of Republika Srpska, Banja Luka

In another set of photographs, Catholic priests crowded around Ante Pavelić. Wartime Bosniak muftis in elaborate headdresses exchanged Nazi salutes. There were five portraits of Serbian Orthodox clergy who were imprisoned in Dachau or killed in cold blood in 1941. I climbed the stairs to the second floor, past more grainy photographs of Ustaše victims. I kept walking but could find no mention of the early 90s wars in Bosnia, no reference to Omarska or Tomasica, not even a footnote hinting at the violence committed in the name of Bosnian Serb nationhood. The museum was a paean to the 'retrospective illusion' of the Bosnian Serb nation; no other could intrude. Churchill might well be right. History is written by the winners but how they compose their story says a lot about both their victory and themselves. Denying your past is a sign of weakness, not strength.

During the 1992–95 war, Bosnian Serb forces destroyed all 16 of Banja Luka's mosques. UNESCO protection did not save the most famous of these, the Ottoman-era Ferhadija. Serb militias came on 6 May 1993. Two days later the mosque lay in ruins.

The Ferhadija is now being rebuilt. Scaffolding surrounds the entire building, save the slender white minaret, and it is largely hidden from the city centre by heavy fencing. The day I visited, the gate on the corner of the grounds was ajar. I slipped in and stood staring at the mosque. A tall, thin man in blue overalls covered in white dust beckoned me over to the main entrance. Gingerly I crossed the threshold. Inside a whirr of sanders sang out from the upper levels. I was worried about being hit by falling masonry. A black and white photograph was tacked onto the white stone on the ground floor, it showed three men, one wearing a shawl, sitting on the floor. This had been the main prayer room. I stepped back outside, as much for air as anything else. A plaque, in English, said that 'the burial ground and boundary wall were razed to the ground' in September 1993. Another workman stopped as I was reading.

'Where you from?'

'*Irska*'.

He smiled. He and his colleagues were all from Sarajevo.

'When will you be finished, with all this?' I asked, with a theatrical sweep of my arm.

He shrugged his shoulders. 'Who knows.'

* * *

President Dodik never responded to my request for an interview. Long before I boarded the slow train to Sarajevo I realised that he never would. April was turning into May. The crisis in Ukraine was gathering pace. Russia, the traditional ally of Serbia and Serbian interests, was back on the world stage. The Bosnian Serb leader had nothing to gain from an article in the British press about his independence sabre-rattling. Instead I was left to build an impression of the man in his absence, by the way some people spoke about his cunning and his willingness to stand up for the Serb people, and others curled their lips at the very mention of his name.

'Dodik only looks after himself,' an environmental activist told me over coffee on my last morning in Banja Luka. 'If we became a Muslim country, I'm sure Dodik would become an Imam. He's that kind of guy.'

After I left, the rain in Bosnia got worse, much worse. Three months worth fell in just three days. This unprecedented deluge triggered widespread flooding and landslides. At least 24 died, although the real figure was almost certainly higher. One million people, a quarter of the population, were forced from their homes. In Tuzla Canton alone 1,500 landslides were reported. These landslides buried houses and people and shifted unexploded mines from the war. Tennis star Novak Djokovic criticised the lack of international coverage of the floods.

'This is the biggest flood that I've ever seen and maybe that Europe has ever seen. This is incredible,' he told journalists. 'So I hope people can find the common sense and broadcast this a little bit and spread the awareness of what's going on.'

Goran contacted me. 'Can we talk on Skype?'

When I called he spoke so quickly that it was hard to understand him.

'Everything is ruined. It is a complete disaster,' his voice rattled down the internet connection, as if his whole body were shaking. 'We survived the war and now I'm again at zero'.

He emailed me photographs of warped floorboards, peeling paint and dark water stains on walls. It was hard to tell which room was which but the effects of the water were unmistakable. He asked if I could send a message to the 'journalists' association' to highlight his plight. I was not sure what he meant but I said I would do what I could. A few days later I wired Goran half the fee I got for writing a piece about Bosnia. The rest went to a Bosnian NGO in Brčko.

Dodik did not waste time in assigning blame for the floods. The government in Sarajevo was, he said, broadcasting 'Turkish soap operas instead of emergency information'. But even the Bosnian Serb President did express his gratitude to Muslims who came to help their Serb neighbours in the town of Šamac, in the north of Republika Srpska. In Banja Luka a mufti said that during a tour of flood-hit Muslim villages he had come across an 'honourable man, a Serb, who has been rescuing people with his inflatable boat regardless of their ethnicity'. Fans of Red Star Belgrade, long a hotbed of Serb nationalism, tweeted links to emergency efforts in Bosnia.

But as Bosnia's floodwaters receded, questions about the conduct of the relief effort floated to the surface. Dodik was accused of using the floods to strengthen his grip on power, and of sacrificing some areas to the floods to save other, more politically significant territories.

'Dodik is a clown,' Goran told me over Skype one afternoon a few weeks after the worst of the flooding had abated. I had never heard him speak so strongly. Later in the same conversation his sister said that local officials were 'playing politics' instead of allocating aid: 'Our house is like a ghost house now.'

I was reminded of Goran, talking into the darkness, as we drove back through the dark from Omarska. He had said that he had wasted his life. He wanted to leave Bosnia, to go to Canada. But he could not because of his young daughter.

'If it wasn't for her I'd never come back to this place. I would never even think about this place. Never.'

In February 2014, a series of protests broke out across Bosnia. Tens of thousands took to the streets demanding jobs and a better future. The municipality headquarters in Sarajevo was set on fire, as was the government building in Tuzla. But there was little unrest in Republika Srpska. A few hundred veterans and disgruntled residents gathered in Banja Luka, but the rallies quickly ended after Milorad Dodik said the leaders were in the pay of the neighbouring Federation. (He provided no evidence to back up the claim. He did not need to.) Soon the protests in the Federation petered out too.

Dodik and a small cadre around him have amassed huge personal fortunes, but Republika Srpska remains one of the poorest countries in Europe. Average incomes are around £2,500 a year – and falling. Among the young, unemployment is around 50 per cent. Independence is a useful way of distracting attention from corruption, poverty and mismanagement, Srecko Latal, a Balkans analyst based in Sarajevo told me when over Skype when I had returned, empty-handed, to Glasgow.

'Dodik is trying to sell the idea to the people of Republika Srpska that the chance of independence is good enough that they don't need a good job or social services'.

In October, just a few weeks after the referendum in Scotland, Bosnia and Herzegovina held national elections. In the days leading up to the vote there was little or no coverage in the UK press, save a feature on *The Guardian* website asking if Bosnia's was 'the world's most complicated system of government'. The lack of interest in Bosnian electoral politics internationally was shared within the country. Turnout was a record low. In Republika Srpska, Dodik and his misleadingly titled Alliance of Independent Social Democrats saw its support drop but hung on to their post in the state presidency. Just after the elections an audio recording appeared in public in which prime minister Željka Cvijanovic allegedly could be heard talking about how the party had 'bought' the support of two lawmakers in order to ensure a ruling majority. Dodik subsequently proposed Cvijanovic to head the new government.

Dodik's power base has been weakened but he looks set to continue. In many ways, he has no choice. If he left politics he would almost certainly end up in jail on corruption charges. Dodik has the air of a man who would do anything to avoid waking up in a prison cell – even keeping up his incessant demands for the break-up of the most fragile state in Europe.

CHAPTER 6

I Crossed the Minch

Many people in the Outer Islands are Scottish Nationalists. I have always laughed at Scottish Nationalism as a precious affectation of bright young men with a distaste for real politics, but in the islands the concept has more meaning than it has in Edinburgh.

LOUIS MacNEICE, *I Crossed the Minch*, 1938

IN 1937, LOUIS MACNEICE made two journeys to the Western Isles. The Belfast-born, Oxford-educated poet was looking for escape; two years earlier his young wife had left him for a Russian-American graduate student that had been lodging in their home. In the Western Isles, MacNeice was following loosely in the path of Johnson and Boswell, hoping to find 'a wild landscape and a genial people'. The search was largely a fruitless and frustrating one. In the resulting travelogue, the caustic *I Crossed the Minch*, MacNeice apologised for producing:

> A tripper's book written by someone who was disappointed and tantalised by the islands and seduced by them only to be reminded that on that soil he will always be an outsider.

MacNeice first crossed the Minch – the strait separating the Highlands of mainland Scotland from the islands of Lewis and Harris – in April. It was early September, just a week before the independence referendum, when I retraced the poet's footsteps, climbing aboard a hulking Caledonian MacBrayne ferry bound for Stornoway, the largest town on Lewis. The open sea was a plain of unruffled azure. No sign of 'the Blue Men of the Minch', the treacherous aquamarine-hued amphibians that are said to stalk the narrow stretch of sea. An occasional gannet swooped across the line of cameras and smartphones on the ship's observation deck. Behind us was the small town of Ullapool, on the shores of Loch Broom.

The loch slalomed for miles around fingers of land that slinked down off the mountainside. In the distance, hazily, the highest point of an imposing ridge pierced the cloud cover.

MacNeice had travelled north from Glasgow with his lover, the artist Nancy Sharp. (He completely wrote Sharp out of *I Crossed the Minch*.) I made the same journey in the company of a colleague from an Irish newspaper. The previous evening, we almost ran out of fuel for want of a petrol station between Perth and Inverness. On the windy road northwest from the Highland capital skittish deer frequently ran across our headlights in the darkness. We finally arrived in Ullapool around midnight.

I am wary of painting an overly romantic vision of the Highlands and islands. MacNeice himself went 'sparingly with the gilt and the whitewash'. But Ullapool had an undeniable rustic charm. The streets were empty and the harbour was cloaked in a moonlit darkness. Every fishing boat looked as if it were coated in a thin layer of soot. Gulls circled overhead. Perched on an escarpment overlooking the loch was our hotel, the Ceilidh Place. A bright blue Yes Saltire flew from a nearby flagpole. The Ceilidh Place's proprietor is local nationalist MSP Jean Urquhart, who quit the SNP in 2012 over the party's decision to support NATO membership. Urquhart was away campaigning in Sutherland in the very north of the Highlands but her son had waited up for us. He showed me to a fine room with a view of the water and a copy of Edwin Muir's *Scottish Journey* leaning on the bookshelf. As MacNeice noted, many of the 'lions' of 20th-century Scottish literature found a home in the islands: Christopher Grieve (aka Hugh MacDiarmid) spent nine years on the island of Whalsay in Shetland, Eric Linklater always had Orkney and MacNeice himself paid an entertaining visit to Compton Mackenzie's 'exceedingly comfortable' Hebridean bolt hole on Barra.

I woke the following morning to the *Today* programme on Radio 4. The subject of the day was Scotland. Having shown limited interest in the possible break-up of Britain, the UK's political classes were now in a palpitated state over the referendum. A narrowing of opinion polls, evidently, has a similar effect on politicians and journalists as a contraction of the arteries. A few days earlier a poll had given Yes a slender lead. The three Westminster leaders, David Cameron, Ed Miliband and Nick Clegg, were abandoning Prime Minister's Questions en masse and heading north. Scotland needed saving. From itself. Mr Cameron had, the newsreader said, 'issued an emotional plea to save the Union'. That week it seemed that every utterance was either 'emotional' or 'passionate'.

If Ullapool was moved by all this unbidden affection, it was not showing it. As with just about everywhere else in Scotland, Yes posters far outweighed No's in the windows of the town's cottages. On the quayside, Germans in walking boots clutched OS maps. American tourists took selfies framed by green and auburn shaded hillsides. We sat in the car listening to another referendum discussion on the radio. The 'Cal Mac' ferry before us sat with its lower mandible on the dock awaiting the usual diet of cars and trucks. A lion rampant snarled in dark red from a funnel on the ship's deck. The company added the symbol, borrowed from the Royal Banner of Scotland, to their logo in 1965. Back then Scottish nationalists had never won a single general election seat. Now a vote on independence was just days away. A man in grimy overalls beckoned our car forward. In the previous six months my diligent colleague had traversed almost every inch of Scotland reporting on the vote.

'This is the last referendum any of us will get to do properly,' he said we rolled on to the ferry. 'Best enjoy it.'

Stornoway. A name redolent of Lewis' Viking heritage. Stornoway. A name, as MacNeice put in an early entry in his Hebridean journal, that carries with it 'a suggestion of remoteness and adventure', of pasts, Iberian, Celtic and Norse. But, as the town of around 10,000 souls slowly came into focus, it looked neither wild nor secluded. The vast quay, open on three sides, dwarfed the shop fronts and the pebbledash terraced houses scattered along its banks. As the ferry noisily began docking, the mobile phone in my pocket vibrated. The isles – at least their largest settlements – are no longer beyond the reach of telecoms providers. On my voicemail an American radio producer talked quickly.

'We are doing a special about Scotland. We were wondering if you would be available at 6.00am....'

Everybody seemed to be doing 'a special about Scotland' that week. The message ended just as the ferry tannoy called motorists back to their cars. We had arrived.

Stornoway reminded MacNeice of home, of:

> little towns in the North of Ireland, the same streets of grey cemented houses, the same slummy smell, the same sombre women hurrying by the wall in shawls.

Disembarking more than 75 years on, there was no fetid stink or fishwives wrapped in scarves. There is broadband now and a Sabbath-breaking Sunday ferry service. But the dockside, once lively with herring fleets and emigrant ships, looked rather doleful despite

Yes banner, Lewis

the warm sun. Beyond the town, the isle of Lewis itself was flat, remorselessly flat. There were no hills, nothing to catch the eye, save the occasional church spire. Even in the sunshine the town had a drab, melancholic quality reminiscent of Longford, my own native place in Ireland's spongy, boggy centre. Our thoughts are seldom as original as we would like to think.

'No disrespect but this feels like the Midlands,' my journalistic colleague, a Corkman, said as we walked past a row of drab garages and squat warehouses on a road parallel to the shore. The vast, glorious expanse of sky seemed at odds with the mundane built environment with its uniform rows of council houses and half empty retail units.

Stornoway was not, however, immune from referendum fever. In *Stone Voices*, Neal Ascherson recalls travelling to Lewis two weeks before the 1979 devolution referendum. Politically 'nothing was happening,' Ascherson wrote in a contemporary dispatch, 'no campaign of any sort exists, and no information has been sent out.'

The scene ahead of the independence vote could hardly have been more different. Along the pier bright blue Yes signs flapped against every second lamp post. 'Proud Brit Proud Scot' read a poster in an upstairs window of one of the terraced houses overlooking the harbour. A Union Flag fluttered in the breeze. Earlier that month a straw poll taken after a referendum debate in Stornoway had finished in a dead heat: 99 in favour of leaving the 307-year-long union with England, 99 against. A handful of voters were undecided.

At BBC Alba's bright, modern offices on the edge of town we met a chatty local journalist. Over a cup of tea in the Gaelic language television station he ran through the headline issues on the island: emigration, fuel poverty, the removal of tax relief on ferry freight and the ever-present demand for local control of revenue levied on using the seabed. The journalist had been born on the neighbouring isle of Harris, which, rather confusingly, is attached to Lewis, a mountainous ridge forming the boundary between the two 'islands'. After working in Glasgow he had come back to Lewis with his young family,

'You're desperate to fly the nest when you're 16 but then you feel the calling to come home,' he said.

And what would happen in the islands on 18 September, I asked. 'A yes is likely, I think.'

Almost everyone in Glasgow and Edinburgh seemed to assume that 'the Islands' – that most quintessentially Scottish of geopolitical constructs – would be solidly in favour of leaving the Union. As ever, it looked that way on the ground, too. A pop-up Yes shop had opened in an old storefront beside the Criterion Bar on one of Stornoway's narrow streets. Inside sat Alasdair Allan, SNP member of the Scottish Parliament for the Western Isles (which are also known as the Outer Hebrides or *Na h-Eileanan Siar*). Allan was in his early 40s with round spectacles and a thin, almost nervous smile. He was, he said, confident of victory.

'I have been knocking on doors for two years. There has been a real change in mood in the last month.' Unlike the islands' MP, Angus Brendan MacNeil of the SNP, Allan had a reserved, almost sombre manner. He had joined the SNP as a student in the late 1980s, moving to Lewis from the Borders in 2006 specifically to contest the seat. He had even learnt Gaelic to better understand the community he was representing. The tide of the referendum campaign, he said, was turning the nationalists' way, in Lewis and across Scotland. The Prime Minister's appearance in Edinburgh that day would only boost the appeal of independence: 'David Cameron thinks he can turn up here but it could have the opposite effect.' A local SNP councillor, sitting beside him, nodded in agreement. But none of the voters I met on Lewis seemed bothered, one way or the other, about political photo opportunities 300 miles away.

As we spoke, activists drifted in and out of the shop, picking up supplies, eating into a stack of campaign literature and stickers, fuel for their door-to-door canvassing. There was a giant foam Yes sign underneath Allan's desk, and copies of the Marmite blogger Wings Over Scotland's *Wee Blue Book* on a table in the middle of the floor. 'Vote Yes 18.09.14' was painted in blue on the shop window. Not everybody was buying the nationalists' brightly coloured appeal. Next door, an elderly lady sat outside her house drinking tea in the sunshine, a copy of the *Daily Mail* on her lap. Above her door was a homemade poster with a single word: No.

* * *

Reverend Iver Martin leaned back on the couch in the centre of his living room, rested his arms across his chest and sighed gently. The middle-aged minister in the Stornoway Free Church had been speaking for almost half an hour in clipped, measured sentences about everything from Lewis' Gaelic culture to the religious make-up of the Outer Hebrides: the Northern Isles are a fastness of evangelical Presbyterianism, their cousins in the southern islands are mainly Roman Catholics.

'With two differing religious traditions you do get two differing world views,' said Martin.

A friendly man with a warm smile and a dry wit, Martin had been born in Glasgow to Lewis parents but had returned to the island a decade earlier to tend the Stornoway congregation. The conversation turned to the referendum.

'For some people it has really become an obsession,' he said, taking off his glasses and holding them up to the bright morning sunshine that came through the open curtains. 'There will be a continual agitation for some time to come. I don't think that makes for a healthy society.'

Lewis is often depicted as the last redoubt of non-conformist Christianity in Britain. On a drive north from Stornoway we passed a sign outside a windswept Free Presbyterian Church that warned: 'Thy God is Waiting for You'. It was just the kind of austere, uncompromising image that tends to frame the island's very occasional appearances on network television. Protests against the Sunday ferry crossing, opened in 2009, made headlines, putatively confirming Lewis' Presbyterian majority as dour, backward and resistant to change. But the reality is far more complex, certainly more so than the clichéd vision of 'a hell-fire sermon in Gaelic' summoned up by MacNeice in a second hand account of island religion.

'The tradition I represent is not afraid of debate, not afraid of openness and honesty,' said Reverend Martin. On the bookcase behind him sat copies of Marxist historian Eric Hobsbawn's *Age of Extremes* and *The God Delusion* by Richard Dawkins. In 2012, the minister challenged Dawkins to a public debate when the Oxford scientist visited Lewis for a book festival. The atheist demurred. Below framed photographs of Martin's smiling grandchildren was a copy of Bob Dylan's *Chronicles: Volume One*.

The genesis of Lewis' evangelical revival has often been attributed to Reverend MacLeod, who began preaching in Uig in 1824. The revival, as it was later in Ulster, came accompanied by fevered scenes of religious ecstasy. On Lewis, people were 'seized with spasms, convulsions, fits, and screaming aloud.' The elders that emerged from the crofts, *na daoine* ('the men'), historian James Hunter wrote, should not:

> be imagined as precursors of the sober-suited clerics one finds in crofting areas today. They were an infinitely more colourful breed.

The religion they preached was vivacious and, literally, awe-inspiring. It was at times a politically radical creed, too. Soon much of Lewis had been 'born again'.

In the two centuries since MacLeod a dizzying number of churches have battled for the souls of the faithful on *Tir an t-soisgeul*, the Land of the Gospel. The Free Church of Scotland (Continuing) emerged from the Great Disruption of 1843, when the Church of Scotland split in a row over the Church's relationship with the state. On Lewis, where opposition had been inflamed by the Kirk's willingness to appoint ministers over the heads of their congregations, many left for the new Free Church. Later on came the Free

Presbyterian Church of Scotland, then the Associated Presbyterian Church and, most recently, the Free Church of Scotland. These offshoots, which all have places of worship on Lewis, would require a chart like the family tree of a European royal family to explain fully. It is not for nothing that in the academic literature on the sociology of schism there are two major corpus of empirical research: revolutionary Marxists and Scottish Presbyterians.

Much of Lewis' ecclesiastical landscape was fashioned in the 19th century, at a time when internal church debates often dominated Scottish politics. The Great Disruption was a seminal moment in Scottish political life. It sent aftershocks, too, through the newly created Free Church. In the years that followed, an increasingly vocal section in the Free Church advocated amalgamation with the smaller United Presbyterian Church of Scotland. The leader of this unionism was Robert Rainy, a respected moderator of the Free General Assembly and professor of church history at the University of Edinburgh. The Union had broad popular support, but was bitterly opposed by around two-dozen Free Church ministers, mainly in the Western Isles. Fierce debate raged within the church. The merger went ahead in 1900 but the rump Free Church, derogatorily dubbed the 'Wee Frees' by their unionist opponents, remained obstinately outside. The 'Wee Frees' argued that they owned their church's assets and that in law the new United Free Church was a separate denomination. The House of Lords agreed. The inexorable rightness of the minority – a common refrain in the history of Western Isles Presbyterianism – had been proven.

Despite their well-earned reputation as the most fissile group in the Northern Hemisphere, many Lewis Presbyterians were opposed to what would have been Britain's largest schism in over three centuries: Scotland separating from the United Kingdom.

'I am culturally Scottish and nationally British,' said Free Church Reverend Martin as he sat in his living room. 'To me the Yes campaign are taking away my nationality and making it something exclusively Scottish which I don't want.'

The Churches played only a minor role in Scotland's referendum discussion. The vast majority took a neutral position, although congregations and ministers often adopted individual stances for or against. A few days before the vote, the moderator of the Church of Scotland's general assembly, Reverend John Chalmers, called for reconciliation after the vote.

'All of those who will vote yes and all of those who will vote No, we need to remember that we belong together in the same Scotland,' he said.

Political leaders queued up to endorse the Reverend's words, before swiftly returning to the pugnacious campaign trail. Doctrinal debates were once at the forefront of political life in Scotland, but in 2014 few were taking their cues from the churches. Even on Lewis religion is changing. Church attendances are declining, although not to the same extent as on the mainland.

* * *

The people of Lewis are 'lucky', wrote MacNeice, because 'the soil is not rich and there is no through road for imperialists or globe-trotters'. The land is certainly a hard, demanding one. The entire island sits atop a bed of gneiss, one of the oldest and toughest types of rock found anywhere on earth. A thin, fertile coastal strip rings the outer edges. Across the centre lie flat peat moors speckled red and brown, permeated by small rivers and miniature lochs. This landscape, at times, reminded MacNeice of Iceland where he had travelled the previous year with fellow poet WH Auden. There, he wrote, the lava-fields had 'cured me of the idea that a landscape cannot be too bleak'. He complained frequently of the scenery in the Western Isles.

'Lewis is still not doing it for me,' my colleague said as we drove past yet another marshy field on the uneven road west from Stornoway towards the windward side of the island.

I did not disagree. There was no livestock. The only trace of human habitation was a tumbled down stone wall in the distance. For centuries, a feudal system had held sway on the islands. The situation got markedly worse in the years that followed the failed Jacobite revolution of 1745 (which began when the dashing young pretender Bonnie Prince Charlie set foot on the shores of Eriskay, near the foot of South Uist at the southern tail of the Western Isles). In the 18th and 19th centuries many of the tenants were replaced by sheep during the Highland Clearances. For those that did not emigrate – and often for those that did – life was a struggle. Lewis journalist John MacLeod was not being utterly melodramatic when he wrote in his 1993 jeremiad *No Great Mischief If You Fall: The Highland Experience*:

> We are the survivors. We have to be, we Gaels and Highlanders, for we have lived for many centuries as a tribe on the edge of a rich and powerful civilization which has long viewed us with indifference.

That indifference between metropole and margins is, of course, often mutual. It was Thursday 11 September. On that day, 17 years earlier, the Western Isles – and the rest of Scotland – had voted Yes to the establishment of a devolved Scottish parliament. In Barcelona, hundreds of thousands of demonstrators were on the street calling for a referendum on Catalan independence. On Lewis, little seemed to stir. There wasn't even a fresh breeze to invigorate the senses, just a heavy fug that sat over the island, suffocating it. Like MacNeice, I was now complaining about the Lewis weather.

* * *

> Fish and tweed are the chief businesses of Stornoway. Lately there has been a big change in the method of tweed manufacture.
>
> LOUIS MACNEICE, *I Crossed the Minch*

The village of Shawbost sits on the west side of Lewis, where bog gives way to sea cliffs and isolated sandy beaches. When MacNeice visited Shawbost, a name that means 'Steading By the Sea', the roads were lined with 'Blackhouses', dry stonewalled, thatch-roofed huts in which animals and people often lived side by side. Most of the Blackhouses are gone; some of those that do remain have been converted into holiday cottages. In a well-kept front garden on the main road a large Union Flag was draped around a purple 'No Thanks' placard. A Royal Bank of Scotland mobile bank sat by the side of the road. The scene reminded me of the west of Ireland but without the ubiquitous pubs that double up as shops, post offices and presbyteries. There was little sign of commercial life of any character, save half a dozen corrugated roofed warehouses lined up in a row like milking sheds. Inside was one of the island's largest employers, the Shawbost Harris Tweed mill.

As in MacNeice's day, Shawbost is a weaving centre. The Harris Tweed mill at Shawbost is the biggest in the Outer Hebrides. The fishing trade has largely collapsed but Harris Tweed remains the island's biggest export – after its people. In accordance with a 1993 Act of Parliament, cloth that carries Harris Tweed's distinctive orb-shaped insignia must be made from pure virgin wool produced in Scotland, spun, dyed, and finished in the Outer Hebrides and hand-woven by islanders in their own home.

The social and cultural story of Harris Tweed is not so clearly delineated. Like much of the lore that swirls around the Highlands, tweed is a potent fusion of fact and fable. For centuries islanders had woven cloth by hand on wooden looms, producing heavy garments ideal for warding off harsh winters. Surplus cloth was traded or bartered. What turned this homespun chore into an industry was actually the advent of the machine. As factory production became the norm in the UK, the romantic image of crofters spinning yarns in their cottages caught the fancy of Victorian philanthropists. Lady Dunmore, whose family bought the island of Harris in 1834, was instrumental in developing a market for tweed in London, where it became the accessory of choice at sporting events. As demand grew, so did production. Crofters began dedicating less time to tending the land and more hours to their looms. Commercial weavers opened on South Uist and Barra. By the early years of the 20th century, Lewis had become the centre for Harris Tweed production. The Harris Tweed industry's fortunes waxed and waned in the intervening century but currently its stock is high. Madonna and Gwyneth Paltrow are among the celebrities recently spotted stepping out in Harris checks and limited edition tweed Nike trainers.

'The great thing about Harris Tweed is the name registers. In most parts of the world Harris Tweed gets you across the door,' said Brian Wilson, the Shawbost mill's chairman.

We sat in a large sales room, on chairs covered in herringbone patterns. Wilson, a short man with an intense stare, was casually dressed; a pair of suede shoes, an unfussy shirt, a Harris Tweed jacket. He was a walking endorsement for his unique product.

'If this could be made in China it would be made in China, but it can't be made in China and called Harris Tweed,' said Wilson.

Beyond the busy walls of the Shawbost mill – where I later watched nimble-fingered workers dissect reams of cloth and feed loud, hungry machines – I heard grumblings about pay. Weavers were not getting enough money for their labour, I was told more than once. Wages were low despite the industry's upswing. Such protestations about weaver's working conditions are not new. MacNeice complained about tyrannical mill owners imposing unreasonable demands on the weavers. (Although the poet was more concerned about the disappearance of their spinning and *waulking* songs than their salaries.) Nevertheless on Lewis, I met few people who disputed that Brian Wilson had helped revive an industry that looked to be on its knees just half a decade earlier.

In 2006, a Yorkshire textiles magnate, Brian Haggas, bought the largest mill on the island, in Stornoway. The adroitly named Haggas had a plan: to cut tweed production to just four designs and tightly limit the number of tweeds produced. The strategy was a disaster. The bottom fell out of the market. Many weavers lost their jobs or saw their incomes drop dramatically. (The mill at Shawbost was mothballed before Wilson and a group of investors took it over in

2008.) Tweed seems to invite such grand folly. Perhaps the Walter Scott-inspired visions of noble Celts and proud clan chiefs are to blame. American anthropologist Susan Parman recounted a cautionary tale about Elizabeth Perrins, a bibulous former model who tried to reinvent Harris Tweed. Perrins, widow of 'Captain' Perrins of Worcester Sauce fame, thought it a splendid idea to make evening gowns in thinly woven tweed. Drunk one evening she placed an order for 2,000 pieces. In Storno-

Shawbost Harris Tweed mill

way, crofter-weavers worked overtime to supply this unexpected surge in demand. Development agencies talked up a new golden age for Harris Tweed. But the orders were a chimera. When the weavers demanded payment Ms Perrins' company was wound up.

Brian Wilson, I sensed, would not make such rudimentary business mistakes. A minister in Tony Blair's first Labour government in Westminster and later the then Prime Minister's trade envoy, Wilson has been one of the most beguiling characters in Scottish public life for four decades. Before his parliamentary career he had founded *The West Highland Free Press* in 1972. In its early days, the paper was a constant agitator for reform. In person Wilson was as spikily intelligent as he seemed in his weekly column in *The Scotsman* – and just as lukewarm on devolution and scornful of Scottish nationalists. He called Alex Salmond 'a bully', and decried the SNP as a movement driven by the politics of grievance. Wilson said that a Yes vote would be disastrous for the Harris Tweed industry. (He did not mention that a major investor in the Shawbost mill was oil executive Ian Taylor. In 2013, Taylor made a £500,000 donation to Better Together that sparked widespread controversy amid allegations that his company, Vitol, avoided UK tax and had been engaged in shady business dealings overseas. Taylor denied the claims.)

As with Alasdair Allan, Wilson was confident that his side would win the following week: 'I have to believe that the society I live in is not going to march to the precipice without noticing what is over the edge.'

Wilson complained that the nationalists centralised power in the capital. He cited what he said was a popular saying on Lewis: 'They ignore us in London but hate us in Edinburgh.' Earlier that day someone else had quoted the same phrase to me but with the word order slightly rejigged so that it was Edinburgh that was indifferent, London pernicious.

While on Lewis, MacNeice met the editor of the *Stornoway Gazette*, who told him that 3,000 Lewismen had left the island in the three years after the First World War. On a balmy late summer's evening, I went for dinner with Fred Silver, another erstwhile editor of the same journal. An Englishman with hair the same colour as his name, Silver had lived for more than two decades in the Western Isles. We ate baltis in Stornoway's only Indian restaurant, overlooking the quayside, and talked mainly about the referendum. Although Silver wore a blue Yes badge, he said there was local wariness about whether independence would actually mean more power for the island. He, too, complained about the SNP administration's zeal for centralisation that had brought policing, emergency services and European funding all under central government control. A council tax freeze mandated from Edinburgh had left officials in the pebble-dashed council offices, built in the 1970s to house the then newly created Western Isles local authority, with even less control over local affairs. Recent Public sector cuts had hit the island hard.

'You can actually demonstrate that the best period for the island was under the Tory government in the 1980s,' Silver said, citing the creation of a Gaelic television fund, the spread of Gaelic medium education and the establishment of a local enterprise company that has since been disbanded. 'Thatcher's subsidiarity was actually really radical.'

For many on Lewis, the independence referendum was less about currency or European Union membership than what the islands would gain either from staying with the UK or in an independent Scotland. In 2013, the Western Isles teamed up with Scotland's two northerly island chains, Shetland and Orkney, as part of the 'Our Islands, Our Future' campaign, in an effort to secure a better deal for island communities whatever way the vote went. The Scottish Government proposed handing over to the islands control of all income from leasing the seabed for wind farms, piers and boats moorings – money that currently goes to the UK's Crown Estate – and the devolution of planning to local partnerships. Westminster's offer was nominally confidential but had circulated locally. It was widely held in poor esteem. One Lewis journalist dismissed the proposal from London as 'nothing more than an office and a phone line'.

The Western Isles certainly needs a new, more tailored economic strategy. The islands are among the most deprived places in the UK. Average incomes are only around 70 per cent of those in the rest of the country, and fuel poverty rates are the highest in Western Europe. In the 1930s, when MacNeice visited, the situation was not all that different – the primary reason why so many Lewis men and women emigrated, as they still do. MacNeice was not a natural social scientist and when he did mention economic matters, often in passing, he tended to blame the islanders themselves for their material condition. They were by turns lazy, lacking entrepreneurial spirit and corrupted by 'the fussy mentality of Glasgow and the jerky culture of an English public library'. Any suggestion that the islands could be economically self-supporting was 'absurd', and their only possible salvation, MacNeice concluded, lay in attracting rich outsiders seeking solace from the din of modernity.

> The islands perhaps can be saved if they are turned into rest-care stations for people from the world of success, but it is doubtful if

this will save the islanders... The natives have not got the money-making conscience.

Despite his snide, borderline racist tone, MacNeice did occasionally acknowledge that – then as now – the islanders could hardly be described as masters of their own economic destiny. Lewis, like much of Scotland, is the product of a land tenure system that still sees land ownership concentrated in the hands of a remarkably small number of people. Over the centuries, numerous owners passed through Lewis, many hoping to exploit the island's resources for profit – often with abysmal results. In 1844, for example, East India company magnate, Sir James Matheson, bought the entire island of Lewis. The sale was funded by the lucrative proceeds from running opium into China. The newly installed laird built Lews Castle, a stately collection of Victorian turrets and decorous ramparts which still stands in Stornoway, separated from the town by a thin sliver of harbour water. Matheson encouraged his tenants, many of whom suffered from the affects of the Irish potato blight, to emigrate to Canada. His business efforts, however, largely failed and in 1919, the Matheson family, in need of cash, sold the island to William Hesketh Lever, founder of Lever Brothers. Lord Leverhulme was not quite an archimperialist – he sat as a Liberal MP and gave generously to charity – but he was a globetrotter, advocating the expansion of his cleaning product empire into Africa and Asia. On purchasing Lewis, the Viscount proclaimed that he would make the island work 'on business lines and we will have nothing to do with philanthropy'. Again, this strategy came to naught. Only a couple of years later, Leverhulme announced that he was leaving – and was offering the land of Lewis to its people. In the end, most of the island, deemed unprofitable by the residents, was parcelled off and sold on the open market.

Times have changed, but not completely. Land ownership remains a thorny issue across the Western Isles, and indeed Scotland. About three-quarters of all private land in the entire country is owned by just 2,500 people. Take a drive almost anywhere beyond the housing schemes of the Central Belt and you will soon run into vast private estates. The Duke of Buccleuch alone owns some quarter of a million acres.

In 2003, the Labour government in Holyrood introduced the Land Reform Act, which allowed local communities to buy the land they live on. While the Act had little impact on baronial estates on the mainland, it transformed many island communities. Since its introduction, around 70 per cent of the Outer Hebrides have come under direct community ownership. Community buy-outs have taken place on Harris and South Uist; the Stornoway Trust still owns the 70,000 acres around the town gifted by Lord Leverhulme in 1923. On Eigg in the Inner Hebrides, the local community raised enough money to buy the entire island. But elsewhere buyouts have been slow. There were complaints that the legislation was cumbersome and bureaucratic, that the Scottish Government needed to do more.

In *The Making of the Crofting Community*, historian James Hunter wrote that Scottish self-government was a *sine qua non* for resolving the land question. But autonomy alone – or even independence – is not sufficient. Political will is needed, too:

> Today the SNP is in government in Edinburgh and could readily give both backing and leadership to communities where community ownership has been achieved as well as to communities where it has still to be accomplished. So far, this has not happened. It is high time that it did.

In November 2014, in her first Programme for Government, Nicola Sturgeon announced 'radical' land reforms. Under the terms of the government's proposals, Scottish ministers would be able to intervene 'where the scale of land ownership or the conduct of a landlord is acting as a barrier to sustainable development'. 'Scotland's land must be an asset that benefits the many, not the few,' the SNP leader and first Minister told Holyrood. The announcement was widely hailed by land reformers and criticised by bodies representing landowners. How the new legislation will work in practice will be closely watched, in the Western Isles and across Scotland.

* * *

'Do you want the Gaelic or the English?' the cherub-faced elder at the entrance to Stornoway Free Church smiled. He held a different copy of the Bible in each hand.

MacNeice had complained that his ignorance in Gaelic left him 'unable to become intimate with the lives of the people' on the islands. I could empathise. My own knowledge of my native tongue is so rusty it could transmit tetanus. I took both Bibles.

'I'll try and follow the Gaelic'.

The elder smiled again. 'Yes, maybe you'll pick up some of it.'

He pointed me into the church, where the weekly Gaelic service was about to commence. I slotted into a pew on the empty left-hand side. Directly opposite sat a row of elderly women. Their fine hats in shades of pinks, blues and greens looked like giant, unwrapped chocolates from the kind of tins that appear as unwanted Christmas gifts. Behind them were another row of women of similar age and sartorial style. The rest of the church was empty bar a solitary gentleman with drooping eyelids, a younger woman in the back row, and me.

The church looked almost impossibly bare, especially to someone who had been raised on weekly trips to a Catholic cathedral studded with stained glass windows and theatrical depictions of Christ in various expressions of discomfort as he carried the cross up the mount. There were no icons to fixate on, no paintings to distract the eye, no chalices or trinkets to reflect the harsh glare of the overhead lights.

The minister entered by a small door, followed by a troop of elders. I had expected Iver Martin, for this was his church, but it was a different preacher, one with a kind, round face. He smiled straight at me.

'Before we start I would like to welcome a guest.' The ladies turned in unison and beamed at me. I may have blushed a little.

'Do you understand Gaelic?' As far as I can remember no one was ever addressed directly from the ambo in Longford cathedral.

'Not really, not anymore'. I was intensely aware of my accent, my voice wavering.

'Don't worry. I will direct you to the readings in English'.

And he did. With both Bibles sitting open on the back of the pew in front of me, I followed as best I could as we moved from Psalms to the Book of Ruth and back again. The soft Gaelic words unspooled into the evening air, familiar enough to be comforting, foreign enough to require a constant eye on the English text.

The highlight of the service was the Gaelic Psalm singing. At seemingly irregular intervals in the service the precentor intoned a line of verse, the congregation following suit, each at their own pace. The result was a joyous wave of sound that rose and fell and sloshed around the small church. I stood wordlessly, alternating between closing eyes as the throaty cacophony reverberated through my head and my hands and staring at the line of old ladies that were producing this passionate, glorious heterophony. I felt the noise washing over me, drowning out everything else. The hair on my arms tingled. I forgot about my deadlines and my meetings. I even, for the first time in months, forgot about the referendum. I was calm.

After the service finished a lady in the row opposite stepped across the aisle and, silently, clasped my hand. The rest of her friends followed suit. I stood for five minutes exchanging warm handshakes before falling into conversation with the last of the churchgoers, a sparkly-eyed woman in a purple bonnet. When she was younger, she said, she often sat up late at night and listened to Radio *na Gaeltachta*, the Irish language station. She spoke fondly of Mary Robinson's 1997 visit to Stornoway, to open an exhibition about St Columba. That day the then Irish President had quoted Sorley MacLean, cited Irish land agitator Michael Davitt and spoke of her hope that, 'we can create an island space for ourselves to celebrate what Scotland and Ireland share.' Mrs Robinson finished her speech by praising the European Union for transforming Ireland by 'allowing us not only to redefine in a healthy way our relationship with our larger neighbour, but to see the worth of what lies at the margin.'

The European Union is now a dividing line in British politics. In May 2014, the rabidly Eurosceptic UK Independence Party (UKIP) won 24 European parliamentary seats in Britain, including one in Scotland. In October, newly elected SNP leader Nicola Sturgeon said that the UK could only leave the EU if a majority in all four constituent nations voted for the move. In the wake of the referendum, Scottish support for the EU rose, with opinion polls showing most Scots in favour of remaining a member. A majority in England wanted to leave.

* * *

A few hours after the Gaelic service ended I went for a walk through Stornoway. Near the harbour front, a girl of about 20 with an English accent asked if I had a lighter for her cigarette. I apologised and asked if there was anywhere still open where I could get something to eat.

'I doubt it. They might sell you some crisps.' She pointed at a bar across the street. Outside people leaned on the windows smoking. The sound of music and raised voices carried on the night air. I fancied a dram.

Stornoway has a reputation for hard drinking. MacNeice, in one of the more acerbic entries wrote, 'Apply whiskey and you will notice the resurgence of the Catholic and the Celt.' I cannot vouch for either the religious persuasion or the ethnic origin of the congregation in the bar that night, but there was definitely a boisterous air. Half of Stornoway seemed crammed into the low-ceilinged saloon. Middle-aged men with harsh faces sat surrounded by half empty pints of lager; glassy-eyed teenage girls sipped colourful drinks in the corner, far from the barman's gaze. The bar itself was three and four deep. I stood on the edge of the heaving throng for a few minutes, pushing here being pulled there, but I got no closer to ordering a drink. Frustrated, I went back out into the nighttime air. The harbour was completely still.

* * *

Our ferry left Stornoway not long after seven in the morning. The sky was a fiery red, and rain fell in heavy droplets that sat on the windscreen as we waited in a long queue to board. Half an hour later, our ship finally pulled out of its bay. My colleague looked relaxed for the first time in days. We drank tea and tapped out stories on our laptops. Slowly, Lewis disappeared over the horizon.

Louis MacNeice found the Western Isles a frustrating place. When the time came to go back to London, he was glad to leave.

'I doubt if I shall ever visit the Western Islands again,' the poet concluded in *I Crossed the Minch*.

I was quite certain that I would return to the Hebrides. But would I be visiting the most westerly archipelago of the United Kingdom or of a newly independent Scotland? The answer came a week later. The Western Isles followed the rest of Scotland, voting to stay in the Union by 53.4 to 46.6 per cent.

CHAPTER 7

Scotland Decides

ON 7 AUGUST 2014, YouGov published an opinion poll that put No on 55 per cent. Just 35 per cent of Scots surveyed said they intended to back independence in the following month's referendum. Just over a week later, the same polling company put Yes on 38, with No at 51. The distance was narrowing – and with a speed that surprised everyone save the most hopeful of Yes supporters. By the end of the month the gap was just six points. As the referendum entered the final straight the two sides were closer than at almost any time during the two-year long campaign. A large part of the reason for the fluidity in the polls was the range of viewpoints evident on the streets – and homes, workplaces and social clubs – of Scotland. For many Scots there was much more to the referendum than a straightforward Yes or No – as the amount of activity across Scotland in the final weeks of the campaign attested.

* * *

On 18 August, exactly one month before the vote, Better Together activists assembled in Glasgow city centre for a press call with former Labour Scotland secretary Douglas Alexander. It was a bright Monday morning. Later that day, at a Scottish Government cabinet meeting in Arbroath, Alex Salmond would invoke the 1320 declaration, pledging a 'Declaration of Opportunity' for a fairer, independent Scotland. No such bombastic historical evocations were being made outside the Sauchiehall Street branch of Marks and Spencer's, however. A group of around 50 pro-union supporters mugged for the cameras. Two big blue letters 'N' and 'O' were silhouetted against a banner for the Glasgow Commonwealth Games that had ended earlier that month. A gaggle of photographers spread across the pedestrianised street snapped away. On either side

Glaswegian shoppers marched by. Some looked disinterested, others bemused. A few stopped to watch.

'I'm for a No, a definite No. There's enough trouble in the world without creating more division,' said James Lawn, who was out shopping with his wife. Both were pensioners, the very demographic the Yes campaign had continually struggled to reach. The economic arguments for independence were not convincing them.

'We're better off in the Union,' said Mr Lawn, before politely bidding me 'good day' and continuing down the hill towards Buchanan Street, his wife by his side.

A little later, a Malaysian housewife said that her 'heart says Yes but the head says No'. She had lived in Glasgow for the previous 16 years.

'If we became independent there would be no turning back.' She furrowed her brow below her headscarf.

Across the street from the flag-waving Union supporters, a busker sat strumming his guitar in the alcove of an empty retail unit. During

Buchanan Street, 18 August 2014

the photo call he had played 'Dawning of the Day' by the Corries, his hoarse voice bellowing the chorus:

O we'll fight for the right and the dawning of the day
When we'll rise again to win our claim for Scottish identity

'Dawning of the Day' had been proposed as an alternative national anthem if Scotland voted for independence. Arthur, the craggy-faced busker, was a definite Yes: 'Nothing to lose, but nothing to gain by voting No.'

A few years earlier, he had emigrated to Portadown in Northern Ireland. Portadown, a monochrome town with a long-standing paramilitary problem, seemed an unlikely destination for someone looking to make a new life. Arthur only lasted three weeks across the water.

'The drink got in the way', he said with a wink. Earlier in life he had been a boilermaker in the Govan shipyards.

'We need to get a bit of pride back into the place, get some industry back, get some boats back.' I left a few coins in his open guitar case.

The main reason I went to the Douglas Alexander press call was not to hear the Labour man – his comments about the need to 'turn majority support into a majority vote' would be printed in every newspaper – but to meet some real-life unionist campaigners. Where the Yes Scotland campaign often seemed to have little idea what its growing legion of grassroots activists were actually doing during the campaign, Better Together had the opposite problem. Spontaneous pro-union campaigning was thin to the point of translucency. Better Together also emitted the stultifying whiff of bromide, and New Labour micro-managerialism. Over the previous months, I made numerous advance requests to accompany pro-union canvassers. All were turned down.

As the assembled crowd with the 'No Thanks' balloons began to break up, I made a beeline for an activist on the edge of the group. I introduced myself. He glared as if I had said something to offend him.

'I'm not talking to you'. He sounded angry.

A moment later, a broad-shouldered Better Together official was standing in front of me: 'I'm sorry but you have to speak to our designated spokesperson.' He didn't look sorry. I nodded.

'Sure, no problem.'

With my uninvited minder out of sight, I slipped through the crowd and struck up a conversation with a trio of younger activists. The most outspoken was a fair-haired 18-year-old Glaswegian called Paddy. He seemed intent on exploding my stereotypes. Paddy possessed the cut-glass, placeless Scottish accent beloved of radio producers. Scottish nationalists, he said, were intent on spending 'taxpayers money to cover up for the fact that they haven't go any'.

Paddy was firmly against the independence referendum, but was hoping for another plebiscite soon – on the UK's membership of the European Union.

'I believe that power should be returned to us from Brussels'.

In the European elections that May Paddy had voted UKIP, along with just over ten per cent of Scots.

Main Street, Coatbridge. 12.00pm Monday 18 August 2014. A 20-something Better Together apparatchik in an expensive-looking pinstripe suit opened a fold-up table and set it down outside St Patrick's Church. He carefully laid out 'No Thanks' badges in blue, green and purple on the table. The whole exercise was meticulously managed. Leaflets in Labour red warned about the dangers of independence. A helium canister appeared from the boot of a nearby car. For a few moments the air was filled with the shrill sound of plastic tightening. He tied balloons to the table, so many that it looked as if it might rise up and float off over the bargain stores and sandwich shops that hugged the main street. Finally, a squat black amplifier, a microphone and two empty plastic dark red Irn Bru crates, upturned, were laid out in front of the table. The young man slipped into the background to make way for the main attraction: another former Labour Scotland secretary, Jim Murphy MP.

Murphy is a lean, wiry man in his late 40s with sharp facial features. A few months later, the Labour MP for East Renfrewshire would be declared 'deliciously old school' by a woman's magazine in a poll of sex symbols. Murphy was particularly effective during the referendum campaign because he understood the need for unionists to engage directly with voters, to take their message to the streets. He would go on to win 'Campaigner of the Year' at *The Spectator*'s annual awards. On Main Street Coatbridge Murphy cut a combative figure. He was on stop number 51 of his '100 Streets' soapbox tour of Central Scotland, standing on upturned Irn Bru crates to coax the masses to back the Union.

'Independence is forever. You can't take it back if you don't like it,' Murphy shouted at passersby. Around him some 60 people were congregated in a semi-circle. A man wearing a bright blue 'No Thanks' badge clapped loudly; towards the back of the crowd, a couple of teenagers shouted 'vote Yes.' Most everyone else was silent and looked rather bored.

If you had beamed in from London – as many of the journalists in Scotland during the last weeks of the referendum campaign had

Jim Murphy in Coatbridge

– the scene on Coatbridge's main street might have looked awfully like a sepia-tinged image of 'old school politics'. Men with flat caps and regional accents having a proper political debate. Lots of heckling and gesticulating. Not a 'Mondeo man' in sight. But the vista was a staged mirage, what French postmodernist philosopher Jean Baudrillard would call a 'simulacrum'. Murphy's Irn Bru crates were a representation of working class Scottish culture dreamed up in a party office and delivered by a man who, like many others in both campaigns, had never held a job outside politics. (Murphy progressed from the National Union of Students to an unexpected Westminster seat in the 1997 landslide.) The speeches Murphy and other local Labour acolytes delivered sang with familiar refrains: Tartan Tories and Ravenscraig, Thatcher and the Poll Tax. They were all preaching to an imagined congregation.

But, in Coatbridge at least, apostasy was on the rise.

'I was a No originally but the more I've heard, it's Yes,' Brian Boyle, a 22-year-old who had come to listen to Jim Murphy on his lunch break told me after the entreaties started to fade out.

'I've not been persuaded at all by the No campaign. They've just been too negative.'

As the crowd slipped away and the Irn Bru crates went back into the car, ready for the next stop on the tour, Jim Murphy remained, verbally sparring with half a dozen teenagers.

'What about the oil?' Shouted the loudest of the group.

'Aye, it's our oil,' came another.

Murphy reacted well to the challenge, offering up figures about deficits and oil revenues, social security and welfare spending. But the youths had no interest in listening.

'Free Scotland', one shouted as he walked off with his hands wedged under the waistband of his white tracksuit bottoms.

I left, too, clutching a copy of a publication called *Referendum News*. On the front page was an attractive woman with blonde hair cradling a newborn baby. 'I WANT THE BEST OF BOTH WORLDS', declared the headline. Inside was a take on the stylised red, beige and blue 2008 Barack Obama poster, but with 'Hope' replaced by 'Nope'. Earlier in the summer, the US president had told a press conference in Brussels that he wanted the UK to be a 'strong, robust, united and effective partner'. The comments were widely interpreted as US backing for a No vote.

* * *

On 28 August, Jim Murphy's referendum roadshow rolled into the Fife town of Kirkcaldy. On a jerky mobile phone video from the event, an almost hoarse Murphy breaks off his delivery to duck out of the way of an egg thrown from a tight crowd of placard-waving independence supporters. Another egg hits him but miraculously does not crack. Finally, a figure walks up behind Murphy. A split second later, dark yellow yolk spills down the back of his white shirt. Murphy continues speaking from atop his Irn Bru crates. (Actually he shouts, 'I will not be silenced by nationalist mobs.') Afterwards Murphy announced that he was taking a break from the '100 Streets' tour in the face of 'sinister' and 'orchestrated' attacks from nationalists.

The self-enforced hiatus lasted about 48 hours. Two weeks before the referendum, Jim Murphy was back on the street, addressing an audience in Glasgow city centre. Earlier that day, Alex Salmond and Nicola Sturgeon had appeared at a huge rally on nearby Buchanan Street. The polls were continuing to narrow. Two days later a seismic poll in *The Sunday Times* would put Yes in front, 51 to 49.

A crowd of around 100 people gathered to hear Jim Murphy speak outside the imposing neo-classical Gallery of Modern Art (GOMA), originally built in the late 18th century as the townhouse of William Cunninghame of Lainshaw, a tobacco lord who made his fortune through the triangular slave trade. As ever, a fluorescent traffic cone sat atop the crown of the equestrian statue of the Duke of Wellington. Below it, Jim Murphy was introduced by Andy Cameron, a white-haired comedian in a pink shirt who had once been a star turn on BBC Scotland. The Labour politician looked relaxed, holding a bottle of water as he warmed to his sales pitch.

'Independence is forever. There are no guarantees. There is no going back.' Some in the crowd cheered, a couple booed. From a building site across the street, a workman shouted 'vote Yes'. A red-faced man with a 'No Thanks' flag roared 'get back to work'. It felt like a stand off between opposing football fans. Near Murphy, a couple of men in Rangers jerseys held a Union Flag.

The biggest round of applause was reserved for a reference to the egg-throwing incident in Kirkcaldy: 'I'm not going to be scared. I'm not going to be intimidated'. There were cheers, too, when Murphy told the audience that No vote could be a patriotic vote: 'You don't have to vote for the break up of our country to prove you're Scottish.'

Among the audience outside the GOMA was Craig Hazlett, who had stopped to listen to Murphy's address on his way home from work as a floorer. Streaks of paint lined his overalls. The 29-year-old seemed unswayed by the political showmanship: 'We have been hearing the same rhetoric from both sides. There is no unbiased opinion,' he said.

Glaswegian artist, Helen, was 'leaning more to No', which, she said made her 'uncool' among her friends. The previous weekend, 1300 Scottish artists, writers and musicians had all come out in favour of independence.

'I feel so confused by both sides that in the end I think I'll end up trusting my gut,' she said. 'I have fears for my parents' generation and for people who are going into retirement.'

I left Jim Murphy arguing with a Yes voter about whether Scotland would be a more socially just place under independence. Around the corner, on Buchanan Street, I passed by my first 'wish tree'. In the months leading up to the referendum, twine and paper wish trees had popped up across Scotland. 'Vote Yes for a Better Future', read a note written in black felt pen on a yellow luggage tag suspended between a pair of saplings on Buchanan Street. Another said: 'Scotland is beautiful keep it that way'.

It was hard at times during the referendum not to feel that the campaign was a clash between harsh realities and idealistic visions of the future. Better Together were well funded and ran a ruthless, at times cynical operation that focused squarely on the dangers of leaving the union. There was nothing cuddly-feely about their teams of well-paid, well-dressed communications professionals, but there was a brutal efficiency to the unionist enterprise. The pro-independence side, on the other hand, was often chaotic and disorganised. Yes Scotland had cash, thanks mainly to the largesse of lottery winners Chris and Colin Weir. But the umbrella organisation created to oversee the wider independence movement was poorly run and riven by personality clashes and internal divisions. During the campaign Yes Scotland was usurped by the SNP, which made the key decisions. And yet, propelled by social media, grassroots Yes groups, often with little or no connection to a central office, sprung up across the country. Journalist Paul Hutcheon estimated that by 18 September there were some 300 pro-independence community groups, 50 sectoral organisations and dozens of spin offs, all holding meetings and canvases, organising voter registration drives – and planting wish trees.

The Buchanan Street wish tree was being tended to by a comparative literature graduate named Aileen McKay, who had been involved with both the pro-independence National Collective and the Radical Independence Campaign. McKay was not being paid by anyone. She could have had little expectation of a job in head office regardless of the referendum result. She had just decided to buy some luggage tags and go out on the street in the sunshine.

'I want to effect a change in my lifetime. I don't see change coming from within the existing structures so we need independence,' she said. As we spoke, a couple of teenage girls stopped to add their wishes to the tree. One wrote simply: 'Yes'.

* * *

The media do not transmit an idea which happens to have been fed into them. It matters precious little what has been fed into them: it is the media themselves, the pervasiveness and importance of abstract, centralized, one to many communication, which itself automatically engenders the core idea of nationalism quite irrespective of what in particular is being put into the specific messages transmitted.

ERNEST GELLNER, *Nations and Nationalism*, 1983

On 25 August, Alex Salmond and Alistair Darling, former Chancellor of the Exchequer and head of the Better Together campaign, met in the last of two televised debates before the referendum. Their first encounter was broadcast live on STV in Scotland, attracting so many viewers online that the channel's internet player crashed. (ITV had decided to show *Alan Titchmarsh: Love Your Garden* on network in England, Wales and Northern Ireland.) The second debate, for the BBC, took place at Glasgow's Kelvingrove Art Gallery and Museum.

On the night of the debate, half a dozen men carrying Union flags stood outside the front steps of Kelvingrove. By the museum's back entrance, an ageing man with a guitar belted out Dougie McLean's 'Caledonia'. A constant nationalist refrain during the campaign, the song had once featured on a commercial for Tennent's lager. A pair of TV cameraman beamed as they panned across a huge banner that said 'End London Rule'.

I made my way past security and into the press gallery, a long, narrow basement chamber in the bowels of Kelvingrove. Political advisors and party hacks from both Yes Scotland and Better Together buzzed around the crowded room. Near the entrance, a queue of journalists waited to speak with the then Labour leader Johann Lamont. Close by, a small huddle congregated around Liberal Democrat MP Danny Alexander. Humza Yousaf, SNP Minister for External Affairs, a post created after the 2011 Holyrood election, stood a few feet away, deep in conversation with a pair of journalists. Towards the back of the room, recognisable faces from national news channels practised their autocues.

I took a seat at one of three long, white benches. A journalist I knew at the next table turned to me: 'I've to file for 10.30pm tonight. I already have a top line – "both sides claim victory in debate".'

But it quickly became apparent that the contest was too one-sided to be declared a score draw. Where Darling was widely seen to have edged the first debate, Alex Salmond was in control of the rematch, exuding a breezy confidence as he ventured out from behind his lectern to deliver florid asides to the surprisingly receptive audience.

As the debate dragged on the apparatchiks in the pressroom grew increasingly nervous. Senior Better Together spindoctors paced around the back of the hall, or, in a flurry of fingers, tapped away on tablets and smartphones. Every few minutes a press officer would arise and sidle over to one of the suite of journalists, whispering furtively into their ear. After the contest ended, the press handlers prowled the room, arguing fiercely that their man had won and fielding questions from journalists. Whether any of this made any impact on the coverage is hard to say: just about every newspaper, regardless of stripe or allegiance, declared Alex Salmond the winner. A snap post-debate poll for *The Guardian* gave the SNP leader victory by 71 points to 29.

Scotland's referendum story was also, a story about the nation's media, about how the campaign was covered. At times the press corps came under as much scrutiny as the politicians. Aggrieved nationalists regularly accused newspapers and broadcasters – 'the mainstream media' – of bias. Alex Salmond often blew dog whistles to his supporters. During a live interview in the final week of the referendum campaign, the First Minister repeatedly told BBC Scotland anchor Jackie Bird he hoped that the BBC would report his comments. The implication was clear to those who wanted to hear it: the BBC and the 'MSM' were biased against independence.

The nationalists' ire is not wholly incomprehensible. While almost 45 per cent of the electorate voted for independence, nearly all the nation's newspapers were opposed. One title, *The Sunday Herald*, adopted a stridently pro-Yes line, especially in the final months of the campaign. (The paper's year-on-year sales apparently doubled in the weeks running to the vote.) Some newspapers did toe a broadly balanced line. In many others, however, every day seemed to bring a fresh 'hammer blow' for Scottish nationalism, which was often personified by Alex Salmond. In the six months up to March 2014, headlines that contained a politician's name featured Salmond

57 per cent of the time, according to research by Dr David Patrick, a Scottish academic based in South Africa. The next closest figure, David Cameron, appeared in one in ten. A year-long study by the University of the West of Scotland released in January 2014 found a significantly greater number of TV news stories deemed favourable to No.

In the final days of the campaign, opposition to leaving the union became increasingly overt in some Scottish and UK newspapers. The weekend before the vote, *The Sunday Telegraph*'s front page featured kilted soldiers carrying a Union-flag draped coffin below the headline:

> Scottish soldiers lost their lives trying to preserve the United Kingdom. What will their families say now: 'Well it no longer matters'?

On the day of the vote *The Times* came with a wraparound red, white and blue cover featuring a quote from Rabbie Burns' 'Auld Lang Syne' on the back and a brief history of the Union on the inside pages. Not every outlet's coverage was as emotive, but editorials urging a No vote appeared in *The Guardian, The Herald, The Scotsman, The Daily Record* as well as in most other daily newspapers.

But to pick out these individual examples is to miss a much wider, more important, point. Media, as celebrated sociologist of nationalism Ernest Gellner understood, plays a pivotal role in producing and sustaining the illusion of the nation-state as a permanent and immutable object. When the nation-state itself is contested – as it is by definition during a referendum on secession – newspapers, radio and television almost unwittingly buttress the status quo, the established nation-state, against the prospective breakaway nation. Even if the BBC had swamped the airwaves with SNP election broadcasts for months ahead of the referendum the very existence of a *British* Broadcasting Corporation was testament to the power of the idea of the United Kingdom as the legitimate nation-state (or, as Tom Nairn has put it, 'state-nation') on the island of Britain. That Scotland has long been accepted as a 'nation' made little difference in this process. State, when it comes to established media, trumps all else. On UK network broadcasts Scottish nationalist voices – by definition in this context anti-statist – were frequently presented as divergent and marginal.

The key difficulty for the media during the referendum was not one of intentional bias but often of an inability to reflect the vivacity of the campaign back to its participants. That is hardly surprising. The 'tablets of stone' model of journalism – spindoctors and party hacks feeding morsels to favoured members of the Fourth Estate, as in the basement in Kelvingrove during the second televised debate – has long held sway in Scotland. Part of the reason for this is financial. Scotland once had the highest newspaper readership levels in Europe. Now, average sales are down as much as ten per cent year-on-year. Morale is low. Job losses are frequent and swingeing. Pagination has been scaled back. Beyond football and the echoey corridors of the Holyrood lobby, many Scottish titles' coverage is increasingly threadbare.

For some papers there were simply not enough journalists to go out and tell the stories of the referendum, so the focus remained on politicians and press releases. That was a boon for Better Together, which comfortably won the 'air war' with a much slicker and effective media strategy. (Yes Scotland's press team, at times, barely seemed even to answer the phone.) *The Financial Times* was widely (and rightly) hailed for the quality of its referendum coverage, which reflected an editorial decision to dedicate large amounts of space and resources to getting under the skin of the story. *The Scotsman*, by contrast, was often chastised by nationalists for its coverage, but the reality was that the paper was operating on severely limited resources. In April 2014, *The Scotsman*, once a globally recognised journalism brand, left its flagship offices near the Parliament at Holyrood, to be replaced by computer games company Rockstar North, makers of *Grand Theft Auto*. On referendum night, *The Scotsman* had just three reporters covering the entire country. Just weeks after the vote, Johnston Press, the heavily indebted owners of *The Scotsman*, announced significant job losses at its Edinburgh titles.

But economics was not the only reason why Scotland's media often struggled to tell the independence story. Most Scottish newspaper readers are middle class, a constituency that remained largely unmoved by the nationalist offering. Most journalists were giving their readers what they wanted. Or at least what those readers that remained wanted. (Frequent sniping at members of the press on social media by independence supporters did little to endear the nationalist cause to print journalists, either). But even before the campaign, many Scots were turning away from established media, increasingly getting their information from alternative sources, especially social media. Audiences, particularly those in favour of independence, were actively seeking out media that reflected their experience of the referendum back to them. Confirmation bias is seldom a good thing, but that independence supporters collectively donated almost £1million to pro-Yes media attests to a genuine depth of feeling. A plethora of new ventures attracted hundreds of thousands of readers: the controversial *Wings Over Scotland*, *Bella Caledonia*, and *Newsnet Scotland* (for which, in the interests of full disclosure, I was an occasional paid contributor during the last six months of the referendum).

Much of the criticism of the media during the referendum focused on the BBC. This was not always justified, but in the main the corporation, a leading Scottish journalist and media commentator told me after the vote: 'weren't engaged with their audience and they fell into the trap that they were accused of being, part of the establishment.' The problem was not bias, it was 'death by a thousand guidelines' and an inability to react creatively to the internet's disruptive technology. Heavy criticism of BBC Scotland from nationalists, including Alex Salmond, in the early days of the campaign had the effect of making journalists timid, afraid of making mistakes. Nervousness begot paralysis. Often formats lacked imagination. Many leading BBC Scotland journalists had performed strongly in the lead-up to the referendum, but in the final weeks of the campaign some UK and Westminster correspondents often unwittingly repeated government lines, further stoking nationalist anger. The BBC found itself in increasingly difficult positions. When, the weekend before 18 September, thousands of Saltire-waving protesters chose to surround BBC Scotland's headquarters at Pacific Quay in Glasgow rather than canvas swing areas, the BBC responded by largely ignoring the story. Once again, the opportunity for engagement with the audience was not taken.

'Scotland has a national political system but is in danger of losing a national media,' journalist Iain Macwhirter wrote in a gloomy essay on the state of the Scottish press in spring 2014. The referendum campaign bore out Macwhirter's fears. Often hard questions were not asked, neither of nationalists nor unionists. Too much coverage relied on insider information, press releases and blunt data, too little on thoughtful storytelling. Vast swathes of the electorate felt that their voices and opinions were not being listened to. They were probably right. But the referendum revealed something even more worrying about Scotland's deracinated media: it increasingly lacks the resources and the inclination to hold power to account. With new powers for the Scottish parliament in the offing, many are calling for the devolution of broadcasting, but that alone is unlikely to be a panacea for the numerous ills afflicting Scotland's media. Neither is the upsurge in nationalist oriented media outlets. Scotland was once a powerhouse of quality journalism, now the question is how to keep the lights on in the newsroom.

* * *

A pair of young mothers sat drinking lattes in the Platform café in Easterhouse three weeks before the referendum. At a table opposite was Tony Kenny. The Radical Independence Campaign activist was competing with the noise of a whirring coffee machine to explain how an independent Scotland might turn into something a bit closer to a socialist paradise, or at least somewhere less unequal. In 2014, the United Kingdom was the only country in the G7 with wider inequality than in 2000. In Scotland, the richest ten per cent have 900 times the accumulated wealth of the poorest ten per cent.

'In an independent Scotland we have a chance to build social justice, a fair society,' said Kenny, whose family moved to Easterhouse in the 1970s.

Built on the outskirts of Glasgow in the 1950s to accommodate families decanted from the overcrowded slums of the East End, Easterhouse was initially a dream: indoor toilets, open spaces, light and heat. By the 1970s, the 'scheme', had become a byword for urban deprivation, poverty and gang violence.

In 2002, the downtrodden Easterhouse maisonettes even played host to an Iain Duncan Smith 'epiphany'. The sight of a used syringe and a teddy bear in propinquity apparently prompted the then Conservative leader to conceive of the most 'radical' – or draconian, depending on your outlook – changes to welfare provision in modern British political history. The Conservative-Liberal Democrat coalition's 'workfare' policies were born. (The term 'workfare', making benefits conditional on seeking employment, was actually popularised by Richard Nixon in a televised speech in 1969.)

Easterhouse

The bleak Iain Duncan Smith 'walk' past abandoned council flats daubed in graffiti has become something of a pilgrimage for visiting media. But Easterhouse has changed. The old community centre, for years one of the few public services for over 50,000 people, is boarded up. But there are neat rows of newly built semi-detached houses; the Platform café, housed in what was a derelict local school, is a modern venue that often plays host to hipster bands from Glasgow and further afield.

But not everything is OK in Easterhouse. Unemployment is well above the national average. As many people are underemployed, working less hours than they want in jobs that they are overqualified for. The gangs that once dominated the sprawling estate are gone but substance abuse and addiction remain.

Easterhouse voted Labour for decades but on ever diminishing turnouts. During the referendum, the Yes campaign, and particularly the Radical Independence Campaign (RIC), specifically targeted areas such as Easterhouse. Even when polls consistently gave No a commanding lead, the poorest Scots were the most likely to support independence – if they could be persuaded to the ballot box.

'RIC are targeting people who don't normally vote or who have been hit by the austerity and the cuts,' said Tony Kenny as we walked through the estate.

Alongside him was Liam McLaughlan, an eloquent 18-year-old RIC activist. McLaughlan, who wore a white tracksuit and spoke quickly, was converted to the Yes cause after researching a presentation about Scottish independence in his secondary school in 2011. Now he divided his time between a part-time job and political campaigning. Like many in Easterhouse, he had first hand experience of the coalition's welfare reforms: his mother, who earned just £200 for a 30-hour week as a chambermaid in a local hotel, had recently had her housing benefit stopped.

Later that afternoon I called into the headquarters of a local community group called Family Action Rogerfield and Easterhouse. FARE is based in Bannatyne House, a modern, purpose built centre named after the *Dragon's Den* impresario who helped fund it. Despite the shiny surroundings, there was a basket in the lobby overflowing with donations for the local food bank. Inside I met Ian Montague, a tireless former school principal who had grown up in Easterhouse in the 1950s and now spends his days working to improve the lives of its people. Politicians, he said, have lacked the drive and vision to deliver what Easterhouse needs most: jobs. But that could change if people started to find a new voice on the back of the independence campaign.

'The political class are allowed to do what they do because the rest of us don't engage,' Montague said. 'If the referendum only achieves one thing, I think that one thing will be that it has engaged people.'

On 18 September, I met Tony Kenny again, this time at the train station in Easterhouse. We drove to a nearby polling station.

'I'm feeling confident, I think we can do this,' Kenny said as we pulled into the car park of the St Rose of Lima primary school on the edge of Easterhouse. In the back of the small car was a socialist activist from Dublin and a Frenchman who had been converted to the Scottish independence cause after stumbling across a website called 'Celts for Independence'.

In the spring of 2014, I had spent a cold evening with RIC canvassers in Easterhouse. I had been surprised by how many residents were intending to vote Yes – and how many said they were not intending to vote at all. But by midday the St Rose of Lima polling station was on course for a record turnout. Just after lunch, a steadily growing chorus came from behind the metal fence that surrounded the school perimeter. Seconds later a cavalcade of mothers pushing prams turned up the path to the polling station. In unison they sang 'Flower of Scotland'. Some wore Yes t-shirts and badges, and waved flags as small children ran among their buggies.

'These past few weeks I think Scotland's found a voice. We know now that we don't have to settle for what the government gives us,' said Tracy, a mother who had organised the group to come en masse to vote.

'Scotland is going to be very different tomorrow either way. If it's a No vote it gives these kids the chance to say, "we can do it". If we don't do it they will.'

Glasgow Provan, which includes Easterhouse, recorded one of the largest Yes votes in Scotland. There were 25, 217 votes for independence, 19,046 for staying in the Union. Turnout was 74 per cent, more than double that of the 2011 Scottish Parliament election. The local MP, Labour's Margaret Curran, had been among the most visible No campaigners during the referendum.

* * *

Easterhouse, of course, was the exception. The vast majority of Scotland said No to independence. In late August, I spent an instructive evening with Yes canvassers in the Glasgow suburb of Bishopbriggs. The streets were lined with neatly manicured lawns, and pebble-dashed semi-detached houses. There was little sign of the referendum. Unlike other parts of the city, the living room windows were free of posters; there were no flags or stickers in the backseats of cars. This was the land of 'the quiet No's', softly spoken but firmly against leaving the Union.

Outside one house, the Yes canvassers stood on the step, ready to recite from tightly worded scripts as the front door slowly creaked open.

'I'm here about the independence referendum,' said one activist, holding a clipboard with a 'Yesmo' sheet lined with numbered boxes for recording the respondents' likelihood to support independence. The Yesmo scale went from one to ten.

'Nah, I'm alright,' said a bespectacled man in late middle age.

'Do you need any information?'

'Nah, I've made up my mind. I'm alright.' Slowly, but firmly, the door closed. He was a one.

Even the undecideds in Bishopbriggs were not that inclined towards the Yes canvassers' message. A stylish middle-aged woman with purple-rimmed glass, white hair and a grey mackintosh said she was 'verging towards No'.

'I don't like Salmond. His whole manner is very, very aggressive.' She played with a Doors key-chain in her hand.

'Is there any politician you do like?' asked one of the activists.

'In Scotland?' Her face suggested she found the question faintly ridiculous. 'They're all half-baked.' A pause. 'Maybe Gordon Brown.'

After almost two hours we reached the final house on the 'Yesmo' list. There was a bright red Royal Mail van parked outside. A man in the same t-shirt opened the door: 'I'm No but could be convinced otherwise.'

For almost half an hour in the creeping cold, the canvassers fielded questions about the currency and the future of the post office, welfare spending and the army. Halfway through the postman's wife appeared.

'Who is going to pay for childcare for all over-ones? I don't want to pay for someone to sit on their backside and watch Jeremy Kyle.' The SNP White Paper unveiled in November 2013 promised a 'revolution' in free childcare.

'It's all very woolly,' she said, shaking her head.

As we left, one of the canvassers totted up the scores in the rapidly fading light. No: seven. Undecideds: three. Yes: zero.

On Monday 15 September, the former Labour Home Secretary John Reid and then leader of Scottish Labour Johann Lamont held a photo-op with shipyard workers and union leaders on the Clyde, directly across from BAE Systems' Govan yard. On a dreich morning, Lamont and Reid descended from a bus called 'the Indyref Express' to be met by banks of press and party functionaries in matching blue Better Together rainwear. It felt very New Labour, or *The Thick of It*, or both. Reid did most of the talking. Only a No vote, he said, could guarantee jobs on the Clyde. Afterwards I grabbed a word with a 'continuous improvement coach' at BAE, the defence contractor that is by now just about the only major employer on the Clyde. He was voting No, but not because he thought he would lose his job if Scotland became independent.

'I'm saying no to division. I don't like the concept of nationalism,' he said.

That Monday night, Tom Nairn, who for so long provided the intellectual ballast to the Scottish nationalist project, made a rare public appearance, in a haar-enveloped Edinburgh.

> The moment is right for Scotland to have, in a relatively short time, the chance to contribute to nationality politics and not nationalism in the old, traditional sense.

There was lots of passion in the packed room in Edinburgh University's Old College, but there was a feeling, too, that most people were preparing themselves for disappointment.

The following day, just 48 hours before the vote, Scotland woke to news that a No vote would be the precursor to further devolution. 'The Vow' announced on the front page of *The Daily Record* featured a mocked up parchment pledging new powers for Holyrood and signed by David Cameron, Nick Clegg and Ed Miliband, the leaders of the three largest Westminster parties. It is doubtful that 'The Vow' swayed many voters but it contributed to a growing mood that, after a scare in the polls, Scotland would vote to stay in the Union.

The final opinion polls all gave No a slender but consistent lead. And, as the results began to roll in as Thursday 18 September turned to Friday 19, it became apparent that much of Scotland was quietly, but firmly, against independence. The eventual margin of victory – over 55 per cent in favour of staying in the union – was greater than many No supporters had hoped. The battle for Scotland was over – at least for the moment.

Can the Centre Hold?

The crisis consists precisely in the fact that the old is dying and the new cannot be born; in this interregnum a great variety of morbid symptoms appear.

ANTONIO GRAMSCI, Italian Marxist political philosopher,
Selections from the Prison Notebooks, 1971

ON TUESDAY 23 SEPTEMBER 2014 Holyrood's capacious, wood-panelled debating chamber was unusually busy. The public gallery was full for Alex Salmond's first appearance after the referendum. On the floor, most of the parliamentarians were in their seats. As the electronic clock edged past 14:00, Salmond rose to loud applause. Just a few days earlier the First Minister had accepted referendum defeat and announced his intention to resign. Now he smiled as he began to speak.

This has been the greatest democratic experience in Scotland's history and has brought us great credit both nationally and internationally.

Salmond contrasted the previous week's referendum with the messy 1979 devolution vote. While 1979 was 'a botched job', 2014 had, he said, produced in Scotland the most politically engaged electorate in Europe.

'The true guardians of progress are the energised electorate of this nation, who will not brook or tolerate any equivocation or delay,' Salmond told the parliament. He would, he said, 'hold Westminster's feet to the fire' to ensure that the pledge of more powers for Holyrood was met. A few days earlier, Prime Minister David Cameron had appointed Lord Smith of Kelvin, who had overseen the 2014 Glasgow Commonwealth Games, to lead a cross-party commission on further devolution for Scotland. The Smith Commission was charged with producing its recommendations by St Andrew's Day, 30 November 2014, to be turned into draft legislative proposals by January 2015.

The mood in the Scottish Parliament on Alex Salmond's return was in keeping with much of the two-year campaign that had gone before. The First Minister mixed caustic humour with tribal bitterness, kicking out more than once at the media, the 'mainly metropolitan journalists'. Opposition leaders queued up to perform the reverse Mark Anthony: ostensibly coming to praise Salmond on his valedictory lap, but trying to bury him in the process. The then Scottish Labour leader Johann Lamont criticised the 'intimidating behaviour' of some independence campaigners. Salmond turned his chair and looked on balefully as Conservative leader Ruth Davidson began by saying that she was just eight years of age when the SNP leader was first elected to Westminster in 1987 and ended up excoriating nationalists for an obsession with Scotland's constitutional status. As Conservatives banged their desks, the presiding officer called first for 'silence' before letting out a plaintive, exasperated 'wheesht'.

At least in Holyrood, the new Scottish politics looked a lot like the old.

Scotland after the referendum is a peculiar place. Everything has changed, and everything has stayed the same. Gramscian 'morbid symptoms' abound. Scotland voted to stay in the Union, yet independence supporters reacted as if it were they that had won a comprehensive victory.

In the early hours of Friday 19 September, as the results started to roll in, thousands of Scots opened their laptops and tablets, went on to the websites of pro-independence political parties and clicked 'join'. In less than a week, the SNP had more than 24,000 new members. An emergency hotline had to be set up and a dedicated team assigned to cope with the flood of neophytes. By the time the

nationalists' November conference came around the party's membership stood at over 85,000, comfortably making it the third largest
party in the UK. The Scottish Greens, too, more than tripled in size
in the wake of the referendum. The engagement continued beyond
party politics, too. In October, Women for Independence held its
first national conference, in Perth. It was sold out. Across Scotland,
grassroots groups such the Radical Independence Campaign and the
Common Weal attracted large numbers to post-referendum meetings.

In the lead up to the failed devolution vote in 1979, novelist
William McIlvanney complained volubly about the tedious tenor of
the long debate. 'Passion', he wrote, 'was neutered by boredom'.
Compared with millions on the streets of Barcelona, or armed
independence movements across the world, the 2014 referendum
in Scotland was an understated affair. But behind the subdued
façade, there was an undoubted surge in political activity. Doors
were chapped, conversations were had, posters were blu-tacked
onto windows. As we have seen across the preceding pages, from
the pit villages of West Fife to the housing estates of Easterhouse,
Coatbridge and Dumfries tens of thousands became politically
energised. Many of those who delivered flyers, manned stalls and
tried to convince their friends, neighbours and colleagues to vote
for independence say they intend to stay involved in some form of
political activity.

The SNP has been by the largest beneficiary of this new dispensation. Although the nationalists often struggled to mobilise beyond
their base during the referendum – some 180,000 SNP voters said
No to independence – politically the thousand flowers that bloomed
during the campaign seem to have coalesced almost entirely around
the party. Less than six weeks after the referendum defeat, polls put
the nationalists on course to triumph in both Westminster 2015 and
Holyrood 2016 elections. The SNP, if the polls were accurate, would
increase their Westminster representation an unprecedented nine-
fold, taking almost every Scottish seat and practically wiping out
Labour north of the border.

Such extreme electoral prophecies are unlikely to come to pass, but momentum does seem to be shifting in Scottish public and political life. There has been talk of a cross-party 'Yes Alliance' to contest the May 2015 Westminster election. In Glasgow, there was long a saying that you could shave a monkey and get it elected on a Labour ticket. In the 2010 general election, the odds on Labour holding some Glasgow seats were as short as 500–1 on (if you had £500 on Willie Bain winning Glasgow North East you would have won a solitary pound). Yet, many of these same areas voted Yes on 18 September.

In the referendum's immediate aftermath, Labour, by some distance the biggest players in the successful Better Together campaign, has struggled to reconnect with many of its core supporters. Johann Lamont stepped down just a month after the vote citing 'dinosaurs' in the Westminster party for failing to recognise that 'Scotland has changed forever'. At the time of writing, Jim Murphy, whose Irn Bru crate tour grabbed so many headlines, is widely expected to win the battle to lead Labour in Scotland. Whoever does take over will inherit a party in disarray.

When Alex Salmond took over the SNP in 1990, he said that the party's aim must be:

> to replace Labour as the dominant force in Scottish politics. Our strategic role is to open up the divide between the Labour Party's supporters and its leadership.

This tactic has been wildly successful. The SNP won at Holyrood in 2011 on the back of disenchanted Labour voters. Between 30 and 40 per cent of those who voted Labour in 2010 defied the party and backed independence. Labour now must coax supporters back from the SNP at a time when the social loyalties and antagonisms laid down in the Britain of the 1940s have crumbled to dust in the neo-liberal storm. Their task is Herculean, if not downright Sisyphean. While the SNP has successfully usurped Labour in Scotland as 'the party of social justice' (a claim with varying degrees of veracity), the rightward shift of politics south of the border and an ossified party structure has left Labour flat footed.

The independence referendum did not just expose cracks in the Labour party – it laid bare fissures in Scottish society itself. There was a significant gender gap, with women much less likely to support leaving the UK. In the main, working class Scots supported independence. There were significant regional variations but the Yes vote was highest in deprived areas. The No side, wrote commentator Gerry Hassan:

> carried prosperous, middle class Scotland in part because of fear and anxiety of losing the security, position and even place they had in society.

The task of knitting Scotland back together – if that indeed is what she wants to do – has fallen to Nicola Sturgeon. A solicitor from a working class West of Scotland family, Sturgeon was Salmond's loyal, highly capable deputy before being crowned leader in November 2014. One of her first acts was to announce a nationwide tour to meet the SNP's ever-increasing legion of supporters. More than 20,000 people booked to attend. A phenomenal number in an age, that we are often told, is characterised by political apathy.

Sturgeon has always been a utilitarian nationalist, drawn to independence for what it might allow Scotland to do better. The newly crowned SNP leader used her keynote address at the party's 2014 conference to champion social justice and equality, not just the need to leave the UK. Her speech was widely praised. The following week, glitter cannons exploded as Sturgeon addressed a 12,000-strong nationalist meeting at the SSE Hydro in Glasgow. One commentator compared the event to Woodstock.

And yet often overlooked in the maelstrom of post-referendum Scotland is that the No side actually won, and for good reasons. Nationalists failed to adequately address big-ticket economic questions. Most voters believed that their lives would not be better – and could be significantly worse – in an independent Scotland. Concerns about currency, jobs and even the European Union never fully dissipated even when polls swung in the favour of Yes. Answers to these questions are no closer now, although the calls for another vote on independence rumble on – much to the understandable frustration of many No voters. Alex Salmond said that the referendum was 'a once in a generation opportunity for Scotland.' Some are now asking how long is a generation for Scottish nationalists. Twenty years? Ten years? Three even?

More than three weeks after the referendum, a pro-independence rally was held in Glasgow's George Square. It was a bright Sunday afternoon and the Square looked as it had on those heady September days before the vote. Thousands of supporters waved Yes banners in a riot of blue and white. There were families with smiling children and people with Saltires painted on their faces.

But while the aesthetic was largely the same, the mood in George Square was markedly different. Where less than a month previously homemade signs had declared 'Another Scotland Is Possible', now a trio of mocked-up heads with the faces of Gordon Brown, Ed Miliband and Alistair Darling bobbed above the crowd, with a placard labelling them the '3 stooges' and 'traitors'. A man waved a placard that said '45% My Arse'. Immediately after the referendum, some independence supporters took to calling themselves 'the 45', referring to the percentage of the Yes vote and, in part, the glorious Jacobite failure.

The George Square rally – dubbed 'Hope Over Fear' – was organised by controversial Glaswegian socialist Tommy Sheridan, who had been convicted of perjury but managed to rebuild a public profile and a powerbase in the city on the back of the referendum. A gravelly-voiced Sheridan told supporters that their campaign had only reached 'the end of the beginning'. Many in the crowd believed that the referendum had been 'stolen'. Some meant this metaphorically, referring to the barrage of negative stories warning of impending economic doom that came in the wake of the 51/49 poll in Yes' favour a week and a half before the vote. For some the supposed robbery was literal. But for the vast majority of independence supporters, the vote was fair and legitimate. For many the most pressing post-referendum task was to harness some of the energy that flowed in the months and weeks leading up to the vote.

Just before I left the 'Hope Over Fear' rally I bumped into a friend of a friend, an elderly gentleman who lives near me. He had come with his son and daughter-in-law. The latter waved a Catalan flag. Since the referendum he had, he said, stopped watching UK television. Now he and his wife and most of their friends got their news from Russia Today. There may not be too many Scots flicking on Kremlin-funded satellite channels but the breakdown in trust with the media among a large swathe of society is real. This should be a genuine cause for concern. As long as audiences continue to flee what is left of the Scottish media, its capacity to act as a democratic watchdog will further recede.

There are wider dangers, too, from this inchoate new normal in Scotland. If everything becomes refracted through the 'national question', the dull but vital business of quotidian politics can grind to a halt (for proof, just glance across the Irish Sea to the Stormont Assembly). Scottish nationalists have been accused of seeking to endlessly replay the referendum. Former SNP deputy leader Jim Sillars tweeted that 'majority votes and seats at Holyrood 2016' would be sufficient mandate to declare independence. The SNP and Scotland have become interchangeable in many party dispatches, as if to suggest that what is good for the party is necessarily good for the nation. Whether the deluge of new members will be willing to toe the party's triangulated, centrist social democratic line remains to be seen, too.

Where Scotland – and 'the Scottish question' – goes from here is not at all clear. While Catalonia continues to protest for the right to hold a vote, and Serb separatists threaten to pull apart Bosnia and Herzegovina, it is Quebec that provides the most prescient international comparison. The French Canadian province held a referendum on independence first in 1980, and then in 1995. The former resulted in a heavy defeat for the Parti Québécois; the latter was incredibly tight: a swing of less than a single percentage point would have seen the establishment of a new independent Quebec state.

Two decades on, Quebec's constitutional question remains unsettled, but there is little sign of a pro-independence majority in the province. Indeed many voters seem wary of another referendum. In spring 2014, less than six months before the Scottish vote, the Parti Québécois minority government in Quebec City called snap elections. PQ was riding high in the polls. Voters perceived this as a sign that the party was intending a third referendum. They responded by voting the separatists out of office.

Scotland could end up in similar territory. Another referendum is certainly a possibility. If, for example, the UK was to vote to leave the European Union and Scots voted to remain – a not wholly unlikely scenario – a nationalist government in Holyrood could quite conceivably call another referendum. The precedent has been set.

There is, of course, another option, reform of the United Kingdom. In the last month of the campaign, as unionist bottom lips began to quiver, Gordon Brown promised that after a No vote the UK 'would be moving quite close to something near to federalism in a country where 85 per cent of the population is from one nation.' Federalism has grown in popularity precisely as the polarisation between the status quo and a Nairnian break-up of Britain has widened. Historian Linda Colley has proposed establishing an English parliament in 'a more openly federal system'.

> The Westminster Parliament could remain as an arena for determining major cross-border issues such as foreign policy, defence, macros-economic strategy, climate control, etc., but a great deal of power, decision making and taxation would have to be devolved to the four national parliaments *and* to local and regional authorities.

Federalism, however, still looks awfully like metropolitan wish fulfilment. England, the elephant that Scotland is in bed with for the foreseeable future, has shown little enthusiasm for regional government (as anyone involved with the disastrous 2004 referendum on a Northeast assembly can attest). Neither Conservatives nor Labour have much interest in wholesale devolution away from Westminster. (Just as the devolved governments themselves have shown little enthusiasm for pushing power out from the centre to local levels.)

The Smith Commission faced a number of hurdles. The timescale for agreement was incredibly tight. The three separate devolution plans presented by the UK parties during the summer differed significantly, with Labour's particularly timorous. David Cameron, eyeing a political opportunity to cause serious discomfit for the opposition Labour Party just months away from a UK general election, said that any deal for Scotland would require a solution to the 'West Lothian question', or, as it came to be known, 'English Votes for English laws' (the acronym, EVEL, seemed intentionally malevolent). An arrangement to prevent non-English MPs in Westminster voting on issues that only affect England would little harm the Tory Party, with its meagre Scottish support, but would be anathema to Labour and its sizeable Scottish contingent.

At the end of November, the Smith Commission announced its proposals. Control over income tax rates and bands would be devolved to Holyrood, alongside various aspects of welfare. Unionists proclaimed it a 'historic deal for Scotland'; independence supporters said it had not gone far enough. Michael Keating, chair of Scottish politics at Aberdeen University, described the outcome as 'the minimum the unionist parties could do to retain credibility'. There was criticism that the Smith deal was hammered out by politicians in a room, rather than engaging with the people of Scotland. Almost as soon as the proposals were published, there were reports of more extensive powers being dropped late in the negotiations.

Whether all the Smith Commission recommendations eventually make it into legislation could depend on the make-up of the

Westminster parliament after May 2015. Nevertheless, any perceived sluggishness in transferring fresh powers will be pounced on as evidence of Albion's continuing perfidy. But, for many of those who voted Yes on 18 September, further competencies for Holyrood will be no substitute for full independence. 'The 45' will continue to sabre-rattle for another vote – or even a unilateral declaration of independence – all the while alienating many of those No voters who fear the prospect of another referendum. Meanwhile, many of the activists that became engaged in the campaign will move on to other causes – poverty, welfare reform, unemployment – while the constitutional question rumbles on, unsettled, in the background

There is a precedent of sorts in British constitutional history for what is happening in Scotland. In 1912, the Liberal Prime Minister Herbert Asquith proposed 'Home Rule All Round' as the solution to the divisive 'Irish Question'. Home Rule bills were passed for Ireland and Scotland, but the First World War delayed their implementation. In 1916, while the Irish Parliamentary Party were encouraging recruits to head to French fields, Edinburgh-born James Connolly was among the leaders of the republican Easter Rising in Dublin. The revolt was a failure but the vicious British response sparked a surge of nationalist sentiment. Sinn Fein routed the Home Rulers in the 1918 election, winning just shy of half of the popular vote and a majority of the Westminster seats. Within four years Ireland was an independent state.

In the weeks after the referendum, both Alex Salmond and Nicola Sturgeon talked of a Scotland 'changed utterly', a conscious echo of W.B. Yeats' poem 'Easter, 1916'. But Scotland in 2014 is a very different country from Ireland more than a century ago. There will be no armed insurrection on Scottish streets. A referendum in the near future would not necessarily yield a different result. Despite the membership spike and the well-attended rallies, nationalists have still to sell a compelling case for leaving the Union to a sceptical electorate. The quiet No's are still quiet No's. But the old order has been shaken and damaged, perhaps irrevocably. If the bricks and mortar of unionism, like the stonework of Rory Stewart's cairn, are gone, what will hold the United Kingdom together? The question of how long a Union state can survive without an existential unionism is unlikely to go away.

Nationhood, wrote political theorist Margaret Canovan, is like a battery, 'a reservoir of power that can slumber for decades and still be available for rapid mobilisation'. The independence campaign recharged formerly inert, long neglected sections of Scottish society. The dynamism of summer 2014 has yet to fade fully. Whether this energy ultimately dissipates or can be turned into new, productive forms will determine the lasting impact of the referendum for Scotland and the UK, and for other aspirant nations.

Further Reading

FOR CLARITY AND flow and to make the book a bit neater and less cluttered, I have defied my inner academic and omitted footnotes in *The People's Referendum*. Instead I have listed references divided by chapter. Again for ease of access, I have only cited books rather than any of the reams of newspaper and magazine articles referred to in the text. If further assistance is required regarding sources or if there are any queries about references, please contact the author.

General

Ascherson, N. 2002, *Stone Voices: the Search for Scotland.* Granta, London (2nd edition), 2002.

Billig, M. *Banal Nationalism.* Sage, London, 1995.

Butler, J. *Gender Trouble: Feminism and the Subversion of Identity.* Routledge, London, 1999.

Colley, L. *Acts of Union and Disunion.* Profile Books, London, 2014.

Davies, N. *Vanished Kingdoms: The History of Half-Forgotten Europe.* Penguin, London (2nd edition), 2012.

Devine, T.M. *The Scottish Nation: 1700–2000.* Penguin, London. 1999.

Gellner, E. *Nations and Nationalism.* Blackwell, Oxford, 1983.

Gray, D. *Stramash: Tackling Scotland's Towns and Teams.* Luath Press, Edinburgh, 2010.

Hassan, G. *Caledonian Dreaming: The Quest for a Different Scotland.* Luath Press, Edinburgh, 2014.

Harvie, C. *A Floating Commonwealth: Politics, Culture, and Technology on Britain's Atlantic Coast, 1860-1930.* Oxford University Press, Oxford.

Harvie, C. *Scotland: A Short History.* Oxford University Press, Oxford, 2002.

Keating, M. *The Independence of Scotland.* Oxford University Press, Oxford, 2009.

Lynch, M. *Scotland: A New History.* Pimlico, London, 1997.

Lynch, P. *SNP: The History of the Scottish National Party.* Welsh Academic Press, Cardiff (2nd edition), 2013.

Macwhirter, I. *Road to Referendum.* Cargo Books, Glasgow, 2014.

Marr, A. *The Battle for Scotland,* Penguin, London, 1992.

Maxwell, S. *Arguing for Independence: Evidence, Risk and the Wicked Issues.* Luath Press, Edinburgh, 2012.

McCrone, D. *Understanding Scotland: The Sociology of a Stateless Nation.* Routledge, London, 1992.

McLean, I., Lodge, G. and Gallagher, J. *Scotland's Choices: The Referendum and What Happens Afterwards.* Edinburgh University Press, Edinburgh, 2013.

Miller, M., Rodger, J. and Dudley Edwards, O. *Tartan Pimps: Gordon Brown, Margaret Thatcher and the New Scotland.* Argyll, Glendaruel, 2010.

Nairn, T. *The Break-Up of Britain: Crisis and Neo-Nationalism.* Verso, London, 1981.

Nairn, T. *The Enchanted Glass: Britain and Its Monarchy.* Vintage, London, 1994.

Robertson, J. *And the Land Lay Still.* Penguin, London, 2010.

Torrance, D. *The Battle for Britain: Scotland and the Independence Referendum.* Biteback, London, 2013.

Wood, I. S. (ed.) *Scotland and Ulster.* Mercat, Edinburgh, 1994.

Big Debate in Little Ireland

Aughey, A. 'Faraway, so close: Scotland from Northern Ireland' in *After Independence*, eds. Hassan, G. and Mitchell, J., Luath Press, Edinburgh, pp. 224–234.

Bissett, A. and McKillop, A. (eds.) *Born Under a Union Flag: Rangers, Britain and Scottish Independence*, Luath Press, Edinburgh, 2014.

Boyle, M. *Metropolitan Anxieties: On the Meaning of the Irish Catholic Adventure in Scotland*. Ashgate, Farnham, 2011.

Gallagher, T. *Divided Scotland: Ethnic Friction and Christian Crisis*. Argyll, Glendaruel, 2013.

Jackson, A. *The Two Unions: Ireland, Scotland and the Survival of the United Kingdom*. Oxford University Press, Oxford, 2011.

Mackay, P. 'Lasting Links: A Long Conversation' in *Irish Pages*, Volume 8, Number 1, 2014.

McKay, S. *Northern Protestants: An Unsettled People*. Blackstaff Press, Belfast, 2000.

Walker, G. 'Empire, Religion and Nationality' in *Scotland and Ulster*, ed. Wood, I. S., Mercat, Edinburgh, 1994.

Wood, I. S. *John Wheatley*. Manchester University Press, Manchester, 1990.

From Rosyth With Love

Boyd, C. and Morrison, J. *Scottish Independence: A Feminist Response*. Word Power Books, Edinburgh, 2014.

Ferguson, R. *Black Diamonds and the Blue Brazil: A Chronicle of Coal, Cowdenbeath and Football*. Famedram, Ellon, 1993.

Foley, J. and Ramand, P. *Yes: The Radical Case for Scottish Independence*, Pluto, London, 2014.

Gall, G. (ed.) *Scotland's Road to Socialism: Time to Choose*. Scottish Left Review Press, Biggar, 2013.

Gorman, M. *A Visit to the Soviet Union: Travels in Moscow, Sochi and Leningrad*. www.thecommonplace-book.com, 2013.

Jack, I. *The Country Formerly Known as Great Britain*. Vintage, London, 2011.

Selkirk, B. *The Life of A Worker*. No date.

The Debatable Lands

Haldane, A. R. B. *The Drove Roads of Scotland*. Birlinn, Edinburgh.

Miller, K. (ed.) *Memoirs of a Modern Scotland*. Faber, London, 1970.

Moffat, A. *The Borders*. Birlinn, Edinburgh, 2007

Moffat, A. *The Reivers: The Story of the Border Reivers*. Birlinn, Edinburgh, 2011.

Murray, J. *Reiver Blues: A New Border Apocalypse*. Newcastle-Upon-Tyne, Flambard, 1996.

Watson, G. *The Border Reivers*. Sandhill Press, Warkworth, 1998.

Catalonia Dreaming

Castro, L., *What's Up with Catalonia?* Catalonia Press, Ashfield, Massachusetts, 2013.

Elclaurer.net, *Keys on the Independence of Catalonia*. Comanegra, Barcelona, 2013.

Hooper, J. *The New Spaniards,* Penguin, London (2nd edition), 2006.

Toibin, C. *Homage to Catalonia*. Simon and Schuster, London, 1990.

Tremlett, G. Ghost of Spain: *Travels Through a Country's Hidden Past*. Faber, London (2nd edition), 2012.

Fear and Loathing in Republika Srpska

Glenny, M. *The Fall of Yugoslavia*. Penguin, London (3rd edition), 1996.

Rieff, D. *Slaughterhouse: Bosnia and the Failure of the West*. Simon and Schuster, New York, 1995.

Silber, L. and Little, A. *Yugoslavia: Death of a Nation*. Penguin, London, 1995.

Vulliamy, E. *The War is Dead, Long Live the War: Bosnia: the Reckoning*. Vintage, London, 2012.

I Crossed the Minch

Hunter, J. *The Making of the Crofting Community*. Birlinn, Edinburgh, 2010.

MacLeod, J. *No Great Mischief If You Fall: The Highland Experience*. Mainstream, Edinburgh, 1993.

MacLeod, J. *When I Heard the Bell: The Loss of the Iolaire*. Birlinn, Edinburgh, 2012.

MacNeice, L. *I Crossed the Minch*, Polygon, Edinburgh, 2007.

Parman, S. Scottish Crofters: *A Historical Ethnography of a Celtic Village*. Wadsworth Publishing, 2004.

Riddoch, L. *Blossom: What Scotland Needs to Flourish*. Luath Press, Edinburgh, 2013.

Wightman, A. *The Poor Had No Lawyers: Who Owns Scotland (and How They Got It)*. Birlinn, Edinburgh, 2013.

Wilkie, J. Metagama: *A Journey from Lewis to the New World*. Birlinn, Edinburgh, 2001.

Scotland Decides

Macwhirter, I. *Democracy in the Dark: The Decline of the Scottish Press and How to Keep the Lights On*. Saltire Society, Edinburgh, 2014.

Schlesinger, P. *Media, State and Nation: Political Violence and Collective Identities*. Sage, London, 1991.

Smith, M. *Paper Lions: The Scottish Press and National Identity*. Polygon, Edinburgh, 1994.

Blossom: What Scotland Needs to Flourish

Lesley Riddoch
ISBN: 978-1-910021-70-5 PBK £11.99

Since the referendum, bystanders have become organisers, followers have become leaders, politics has become creative, women have become assertive, men have learned to facilitate not dominate. Independent action and self-reliance have helped create a 'can-do' approach shared by almost everyone active in Scotland today. Scotland's biggest problems haven't changed. But we have.

Weeding out vital components of Scottish identity from decades of political and social tangle is no mean task, but it's one journalist Lesley Riddoch has undertaken. Dispensing with the tired, yo-yoing jousts over fiscal commissions, Devo Something and EU in-or-out, *Blossom* pinpoints both the buds of growth and the blight that's holding Scotland back. Drawing from its people and history as well as the experience of the Nordic countries, and the author's own passionate and outspoken perspective, this is a plain-speaking but incisive call to restore equality and control to local communities and let Scotland flourish.

A brilliant, moving, well written, informative, important and valuable piece of work.
ELAINE C SMITH

Not so much an intervention in the independence debate as a heartfelt manifesto for a better democracy.
ESTHER BREITENBACH, Scotsman

Caledonian Dreaming: The Quest for a Different Scotland

Gerry Hassan
ISBN: 978-1-910021-32-3 PBK £11.99

Caledonian Dreaming: The Quest for a Different Scotland offers a penetrating and original way forward for Scotland beyond the current independence debate. It identifies the myths of modern Scotland, describes what they say and why they need to be seen as myths. Hassan argues that Scotland is already changing, as traditional institutions and power decline and new forces emerge, and outlines a prospectus for Scotland to become more democratic and to embrace radical and far-reaching change.

Hassan drills down to deeper reasons why the many dysfunctions of British democracy could dog an independent Scotland too. With a non-partisan but beady eye on society both sides of the border, in this clever book here are tougher questions to consider than a mere Yes/No.
POLLY TOYNBEE

A brilliant book unpacking the political narratives that have shaped modern Scotland in order to create a space to imagine anew. A book about Scotland important to anyone, anywhere, dreaming a new world.
STEPHEN DUNCOMBE

There could be no better harbinger of [...] possibilities than this bracing, searching, discomfiting and ultimately exhilarating book.
FINTAN O'TOOLE

100 Days of Hope and Fear

David Torrance

ISBN 978-1-910021-31-6 PBK £9.99

Reading this diary back during the editing process it was clear that, like (Nate) Silver (the US polling guru whose view was that the Yes campaign had virtually no chance of victory), I got a lot of things wrong (including the likely margin of victory) but also many things broadly correct. At least I can plead, as journalists often do, that I was probably right at the time.

What can the people of Scotland – and other aspirant nations – learn from this seismic democratic event? Scotland's independence referendum on 18 September 2014 was the most significant ballot in Scotland's history. The 100 days up to 18 September was the official campaign period and the world's media was watching. David Torrance was there throughout, in front of the cameras, on the radio, in the newspapers, at the debates and gatherings, privy to some of the behind-the-scenes manoeuvrings.

A passionate federalist at heart, described disparagingly by the outgoing First Minister as 'Tory-leaning', Torrance made a valiant attempt to remain 'professionally neutral' throughout. His commentary and analysis, as the campaign went through its many twists and turns, was always insightful, if not always popular.

100 Weeks of Scotland: A Portrait of a Nation on the Verge

Alan McCredie

ISBN: 978-1-910021-60-6 PBK £9.99

100 Weeks of Scotland is a revealing journey into the heart and soul of Scotland in the 100 weeks that led up to the independence referendum in September 2014.

From the signing of the Edinburgh Agreement through to the referendum and its immediate aftermath, this book charts a country in the grip of political debate. *100 Weeks of Scotland* is not simply a political book. It brings together stunning photography and stimulating commentary to capture a country in transition.

It examines Scotland in all its forms from its stunning landscapes to its urban sprawl to, most notably of all, its people as they live their lives in the run up to the most significant democratic event in their country's history. It is a portrait of a nation on the verge of the unknown.

Details of these and other books published by Luath Press can be found at:

www.luath.co.uk

Luath Press Limited
committed to publishing well written books worth reading

LUATH PRESS takes its name from Robert Burns, whose little collie Luath (*Gael.*, swift or nimble) tripped up Jean Armour at a wedding and gave him the chance to speak to the woman who was to be his wife and the abiding love of his life. Burns called one of 'The Twa Dogs' Luath after Cuchullin's hunting dog in Ossian's *Fingal*. Luath Press was established in 1981 in the heart of Burns country, and now resides a few steps up the road from Burns' first lodgings on Edinburgh's Royal Mile. Luath offers you distinctive writing with a hint of unexpected pleasures.

Most bookshops in the UK, the US, Canada, Australia, New Zealand and parts of Europe either carry our books in stock or can order them for you. To order direct from us, please send a £sterling cheque, postal order, international money order or your credit card details (number, address of cardholder and expiry date) to us at the address below. Please add post and packing as follows: UK – £1.00 per delivery address; overseas surface mail – £2.50 per delivery address; overseas airmail – £3.50 for the first book to each delivery address, plus £1.00 for each additional book by airmail to the same address. If your order is a gift, we will happily enclose your card or message at no extra charge.

ILLUSTRATION: IAN KELLAS

Luath Press Limited
543/2 Castlehill
The Royal Mile
Edinburgh EH1 2ND
Scotland
Telephone: 0131 225 4326 (24 hours)
email: sales@luath.co.uk
Website: www.luath.co.uk